ORDNANCE SURVEY
LEISURE GUIDE

YORKSHIRE
DALES

**Produced jointly by the Publications Division of the
Automobile Association and the Ordnance Survey**

Cover: A lonely biker surveys the patchwork quilt of fields above Arkengarthdale. Photo by E A Bowness

Title page: The waterfall at Whitfield Gill, near Askrigg

Opposite: The rolling hills of Upper Swaledale at Thwaite

Introductory page: The River Swale near Healaugh

Editor: Donna Wood

Art editor: Bob Johnson

Design concept by: Dave Austin

Editorial contributors: Geoffrey N Wright (The Story of the Dales, A to Z Gazetteer and Directory), Dr A C Waltham (Limestone Scenery), Laurie Fallows (A Day in the Life of a Dalesman, Recreation in the Dales and Walks in the Yorkshire Dales), Colin Speakman (The Pennine Way through the Dales)

Picture researcher: Wyn Voysey

Original photography: Oliver Mathews

Printed and bound in Great Britain by Purnell Book Production Limited. Member of the BPCC Group.

Maps extracted from the Ordnance Survey's 1:50,000 Landranger Series and reduced to a scale of 1:63,360, 1:25,000 Outdoor Leisure Series, and 1:250,000 Routemaster Series, with the permission of Her Majesty's Stationery Office. Crown Copyright reserved.

Additions to the maps by the Cartographic Dept of The Automobile Association and the Ordnance Survey.

Produced by the Publishing Division of The Automobile Association.

Distributed in the United Kingdom by the Ordnance Survey, Southampton, and the Publishing Division of The Automobile Association, Fanum House, Basingstoke, Hampshire RG21 2EA.

Reprinted 1987, 1988
First Edition 1985

AA ISBN 0 86145 233 X (softback) AA ref 58269
AA ISBN 0 86145 234 8 (hardback) AA ref 58256
OS ISBN 0 319 00158 X (softback)
OS ISBN 0 319 00159 8 (hardback)

Published by The Automobile Association and the Ordnance Survey.

YORKSHIRE DALES

Contents

Using this Book

The entries in the Gazetteer have been carefully selected to reflect the interest and variety of the Dales. For reasons of space, it has not been possible to include every community in the region. Certain towns, like Richmond for example, which are not strictly within the Yorkshire Dales National Park, have been included because of their outstanding importance to the cultural and social life of the area as a whole.

Each entry in the A to Z Gazetteer has the atlas page number on which the place can be found and/or its National Grid reference included under the heading. An explanation of how to use the National Grid is given on page 74.

Beneath many of the entries in the Gazetteer are listed AA recommended hotels, restaurants, garages, camping sites and self-catering accommodation in the immediate vicinity of the place described. Hotels, restaurants and camping sites are also given an AA classification.

HOTELS

1-star	Good hotels and inns generally of small scale and with acceptable facilities and furnishing.
2-star	Hotels offering a higher standard of accommodation, with some private bathrooms/shower; lavatories on all floors; wider choice of food.
3-star	Well-appointed hotels; a good proportion of bedrooms with private bathrooms/showers.
4-star	Exceptionally well-appointed hotels offering a high standard of comfort and service, the majority of bedrooms having private bathrooms/showers.
5-star	Luxury hotels offering the highest international standards.

Hotels often satisfy *some* of the requirements for higher classifications than that awarded.

Red-star	Red stars denote hotels which are considered to be of outstanding merit within their classification.
Country House Hotel	A hotel where a relaxed informal atmosphere prevails. Some of the facilities may differ from those at urban hotels of the same classification.

RESTAURANTS

1-fork	Modest but good restaurant.
2-fork	Restaurant offering a higher standard of comfort than above.
3-fork	Well-appointed restaurant.
4-fork	Exceptionally well-appointed restaurant.
5-fork	Luxury restaurant.
1-rosette	Hotel or restaurant where the cuisine is considered to be of a higher standard than is expected in an establishment within its classification.
2-rosette	Hotel or restaurant offering very much above average food irrespective of the classification.
3-rosette	Hotel or restaurant offering outstanding food, irrespective of classification.

CAMPING SITES

1-pennant	Site licence; 10% of pitches for touring units; site density not more than 30 per acre; 2 separate toilets for each sex per 30 pitches; good quality tapwater; efficient waste disposal; regular cleaning of ablutions block; fire precautions; well-drained ground.
2-pennant	All one-pennant facilities plus: 2 washbasins with hot and cold water for each sex per 30 pitches in separate washrooms; warden available at certain times of the day.
3-pennant	All two-pennant facilities plus: one shower or bath for each sex per 30 pitches, with hot and cold water; electric shaver points and mirrors; all-night lighting of toilet blocks; deep sinks for washing clothes; facilities for buying milk, bread and gas; warden in attendance by day, on call by night.
4-pennant	All three-pennant facilities plus: a higher degree of organisation than one–three pennant sites; attention to landscaping; reception office; late-arrivals enclosure; first aid hut; shop; routes to essential facilities lit after dark; play area; bad weather shelter; hard standing for touring vans.
5-pennant	A comprehensive range of services and equipment; careful landscaping; automatic laundry; public telephone; indoor play facilities for children; extra facilities for recreation; warden in attendance 24 hours per day.

YORKSHIRE DALES •
Introduction

Limestone escarpments, drystone walls, sweeping fells and rushing becks, crags and scars gleaming in the sunlight are all part of the unique Dales landscape described within these pages. Whether you are in search of solitude or the bustle of the busy market towns, this guide will provide the key. It explores the history, traditions and geology of the Dales. It lists and describes the towns, villages and hamlets. Walks and motor tours seek out the hidden corners and the finest scenery. Written entirely by people who live and work in the Yorkshire Dales, backed by the AA's research expertise and the Ordnance Survey's mapping, this guide is equally useful to the faithful who return to the Dales year after year and to the first-time visitor.

The Story of the Dales

J B Priestley once said, 'In all my travels I've never seen a countryside to equal in beauty the Yorkshire Dales. The Dales have never disappointed me.' A more recent writer, James Herriot, describes the occasion when he first realised the magic of the Dales, as he was driving along the unfenced moorland road between Leyburn and Grinton, and stopped to look down into Swaledale. 'I was captivated, completely spellbound and I still am to this day.' What, then, is there about the Yorkshire Dales which casts its spell upon so many who visit the area, what quality makes the Dales unique?

Healaugh's grassed terraces were ploughed by the early Anglian farmers who settled in Swaledale from the 7th century

More than anything else it is a blend of the right ingredients of landscape mixed in the right proportions, painted in the right colours whatever the season, and humanised by the handwork of man over fifty generations. From the eastern margins of the Dales along the edge of the Vale of York the land gradually rises westwards. Moors sweep steadily upwards as long, broad ridges to the high fells of the Pennines where a score of summits reach to over 2000 feet. On their lonely uplands are some of the last primeval wilderness areas of England, with spacious solitude, yet never loneliness. Fresh winds sough and moan through tussocky grass and springy heather, to buffet against dark crags of gritstone or crisp limestone scars. There is nothing quite so penetrating as lashing Pennine rain; there are days of quiet calm, though never of silence, for the sounds of the hills are always present. Nothing is so evocative as the bubbling, liquid mystery of curlew-call, the harsh rasp of grouse, lapwing lament, piping of golden plover, skylark-song or sheep-voices borne along the breeze.

Water is one of the ingredients common to the uplands and the valleys. On the high fells spongy peat and squelching green moss help to generate the moorland becks which tumble and frolic down the fellsides, mingle and meet, and leap over waterfalls into small dark pools, create their own charming gills, and finally join the main rivers. Dozens of separate little dales contribute their individual themes into the whole great symphony of the Dales.

Swaledale is narrow, sinuous, grand and touched with the melancholy of former industry. Wensleydale is broad, green, generously wooded, given added distinction by two noble castles. Wharfedale is sylvan, always lovely, with a benediction bestowed by Bolton Priory. Malhamdale and Ribblesdale embrace the Craven crescent, where the limestone bones of landscape are near the surface, creating cliffs, crags and scars white-gleaming in sunlight, yet having contrasting, cavernous depths beneath the ground. A team of lesser dales, not always traversed by through roads, plays supporting roles – Arkengarthdale, Bishopdale, Colsterdale, Cotterdale, Coverdale, Crummackdale, Dentdale, Garsdale, Grisdale, Littondale and Walden.

Visual harmony

Throughout the Dales there is visual harmony both in the intimate scene or in the wide view from a windy hill. Colour is abundant but always soft and muted, greens and greys and many shades of brown; delicate tints of late-arriving spring, darkening maturity of summer meadows, purple of August heather, russet and silver of bracken and birch after the swallows and swifts have fled southwards. Brightest colours come from sky-reflecting waters of rivers, lakes and lonely tarns, or the scattered accents of wild flowers on limestone pastures and scars.

Stone walls impose their patterned geometry across valley floors or arrow up the sides of fells, white limestone in Craven country, dark sandstone elsewhere. Textures display variety and contrasts – gritstone beneath the hands, soft springiness of sheep's wool, cool water through fingers, and the friendly feel of sheltering walls. Natural scents and smells add their own joys: hay in field and barn, wild thyme on grassy swards, heather in bloom, new-dipped sheep, fungi in autumn woods, wood-smoke.

Man's effect on the landscape

The Yorkshire Dales is a farming landscape. Ice and eroding elements smoothed hillsides and valleys but man has changed the landscape most of all. Revealed in names of its natural features, its villages and hamlets, are twelve centuries of settlement and occupation, now dignified by stone cottages, farms and small houses of Georgian times, scattered along a street, facing across a green, or clustered together in a close community. Strong castles and ruined abbeys recall contrasts of medieval power; churches are long, low and broad, usually more humble than ostentatious. In moorland valleys remote from roads the remains of old workings evoke memories of men's struggle for lead-ore, coal and stone. Green lanes where monks trod, packhorses plodded and stock was driven are now used by walkers and others who find contentment or challenge in high and quiet places.

The rhythm of the seasons

With its soft green turf, limestone scars etching hillsides, the insistent presence of stone walls, stone field barns, and stone farms, this could be nowhere else in England. Only the Yorkshire Dales possess the magic proportions of shapes, lines, colours, textures, sounds, voices and people. Local folk cling to their heritage of the hills, and life in the Dales keeps to the natural rhythm of the seasons – lambing in April, clipping in early July, hay-timing later in the month, tupping in November, foddering during the winter months, and throughout the year the twice-daily demands of milking. Upon this seasonal pattern of life are superimposed the weekly market and the annual show. The changelessness of the pastoral cycle against a background of friendly hills is a satisfying anchorage in a troubled world. People find a warm reassurance in the Yorkshire Dales.

'Dale' is a Norse word for valley, so the area is well-named. Rivers of the main valleys – Swale, Ure, Nidd, Wharfe and Aire flow eastwards or south-eastwards to the Vale of York and the meandering Ouse. A few rivers take the shorter, steeper westwards course from the Pennine watershed, the Rawthey, Clough and Dee joining the Lune near Sedbergh, while the contrary Ribble, flowing southwards, eventually forsakes Yorkshire for Lancashire. Dozens of smaller dales fill out the family group, each an individual, but each with a family likeness. The whole area enjoys a unity given by the common platform of carboniferous rocks, with the Howgills of the north-west imparting a slatey counterpoint. Limestone of the Craven country in the south of the Dales dips gently to the east and north, there to be overlaid by the Yoredale Series of rocks – alternating layers of shale, sandstone and limestone, subsequently topped by Millstone Grit, whose remnants make flat summits to the higher fells, and whose dark moorlands are the wettest and most desolate areas of the Dales.

The Strid becomes a foaming torrent on its rapid course through Wharfedale

It is the strata sequences of the Yoredale Series which are largely responsible for the characteristic scenery of Wharfedale and Wensleydale. The limestones weather as long horizontal scars, while the softer shales above them are easily eroded into flat surfaces. The sandstones, usually hidden beneath the scree debris of the next limestone layer, have provided the good stones for the walls and roofs of most Dales buildings. Above the Yoredales but below the Millstone Grit are thin seams of coal, some of which, particularly around the head of Arkengarthdale and Swaledale, above Bishopdale, Coverdale, Dentdale and Garsdale, have been worked for centuries, the last pit near Tan Hill eventually ceasing in the mid-1930s.

The Ice Age

During the Ice Age that ended about 10,000 BC, snow and ice covered most of the northern hills, only the summits above about 2100 feet remaining ice-free. Glaciers flowed outwards from the high land, along existing valleys, scouring the landscapes, smoothing hillsides, and carrying debris and soil, subsequently spread as boulder-clay on valley-floors – more thickly at their lower ends. Moraines which formed during the retreat of glaciers have provided gravelly sites later chosen as well-drained areas for settlement. The Ice Age also affected soils, formed from the underlying rocks. Limestone soils are well-drained, light, rich in calcium, and yield good pasture with a large variety of plants. Millstone Grit uplands have acid, sandy and peaty soils, with fewer plant species. In Wharfedale and Wensleydale the different rock strata have resulted in a variety of soils, and along the valley sides vegetation tends to be zoned in relation to the strata.

After the Ice Age, with the climate becoming

This Roman road leads over the moors to the fort at Bainbridge

milder and damper, vegetation established itself; in 5000 BC the tree-line was about 1700 feet (as it is now), with birch, hazel, pine, oak, elm, alder and willow clothing the hillsides. By 3000 BC some New Stone Age settlement appears to have existed on lower slopes, and 'henge' sites at Castle Dykes above Aysgarth, and at Yarnbury above Grassington, are evidence of Bronze Age usage about 2000 BC. Small Middle Bronze Age stone circles can be seen at Carperby in Wensleydale, and Appletreewick, Bordley, Embsay and Yockenthwaite in the Wharfedale area. By 100 BC Celts reached the Dales area, mingled with the existing native Brigantine tribes, and established an Iron Age culture, favouring for their pastoral farming the well-drained, limestone soils of the Craven uplands. On Ingleborough's exposed summit plateau is the only Iron Age hill-fort in the Dales, extending over 15 acres and enclosed by a wall 3000 feet long.

The Roman invasion

The Roman occupation of Britain left few marks in the Dales. The most prominent site is the fort of Virosidum on a natural low hill to the east of Bainbridge in Wensleydale, garrisoned almost continuously from 80 AD to about 400 AD. This was linked to the major fort at Lancaster by a road whose course today can be followed, mainly on foot, running south-west from Bainbridge, crossing the fells as a walled lane before descending to the Ribble valley above Gearstones, where it joins the B6255 to Chapel-le-Dale and then follows a minor road to Ingleton. Another Roman road crosses from Bainbridge, by way of Stalling Busk and the Stake, to Cray and Buckden in Wharfedale. The rest of its course to the fort of Olicana (Ilkley) has not been definitely identified.

Today's pattern of settlement was largely established through successive waves of colonisation by Angles, Danes and Norsemen between the 7th and 11th centuries. Early settlement was from the east – placename elements '-ley', '-ham', and '-ton', are pointers to this. Danish colonisers following later tended to in-fill between Anglian villages, with '-by' and '-thorpe' representing their chosen sites. In the 10th century Norse families, moving across the Pennines from their footholds in Cumbria and on the Irish seaboard, infiltrated the upper dales, coming into Arkengarthdale, upper Swaledale above Gunnerside, Wensleydale above Askrigg, Wharfedale above Buckden, as well as the western valleys.

The Norse settlers

Whereas Anglian and Danish settlers kept stock, cultivated the land and tended to live in communities, the Norse settlers brought with them a tradition of pastoral farming, grazing the valley pastures in spring and autumn, moving to higher land during summer months. Their summer shielings were called 'saetrs', an element which appears in the names of hamlets in upper Wensleydale – Appersett, Burtersett, Countersett and Marsett.

Landscape features were important to these Norse farmers who spent so much of their lives on the uplands, and from whom we have derived those evocative names – beck, clint, crag, fell, gill, mere, moss, rigg, scar and tarn – words whose euphony is characteristic both of the western Yorkshire dales and hills and of those of Lakeland. It seems probable that the village greens which we appreciate today at Arncliffe, East Witton, Linton, Redmire, Reeth and West Burton may have originated as central areas in Anglian villages where the community could safely corral its livestock, should danger threaten. A certain amount of Norse influence survives today in the dialect of the Dalesman.

An 18th-century engraving of Bolton Castle

The Norman lords
Norman influence on the Dales landscape was
limited. The great Domesday survey stopped at
the edge of forest land – Reeth, Askrigg,
Starbotton and Stainforth were forest-edge
villages. In the later years of the 12th century the
next settlements up the valleys were built as
foresters' villages – Healaugh in Swaledale,
Bainbridge in Wensleydale, Buckden in
Wharfedale. The new Norman aristocracy set
aside forest land for hunting, applying an early
form of conservation, protecting deer, wild boar
and otter for this specific purpose. From their
great castles at Richmond and Middleham the
Norman lords hunted Arkengarthdale Forest,
Wensleydale Forest and Bishopdale Chase, while
Langstrothdale Chase – still the name given to
upper Wharfedale – was the preserve of the de
Romilles and Cliffords of Skipton Castle.

Monastic landowners
A more peaceful, and from the point of view of
land-use, a more profound, influence on the
Dales landscape was that extending over four
centuries by the monasteries. In 1132 Cistercian
monks founded Fountains Abbey near Ripon, and
twelve years later, Jervaulx Abbey in lower
Wensleydale. Augustinian canons settled at
Bolton Priory in Wharfedale in 1155, and smaller
foundations were established at Coverham,
Easby, Ellerton and Marrick. These, together
with monasteries beyond the Dales area, owned
huge areas of uplands throughout the Dales. The
new monastic landowners brought great farming
and sheep-breeding skills; they successfully
managed their vast estates, running a pastoral
economy through a series of granges, each
responsible to the mother-house, but worked by
lay-brothers and local labour. To a large extent
they laid the foundations not only of the hill-
farming scene of today but much of the present
network of roads and tracks. In addition they
drained marshy land, cleared scrubland, and built
some of the earliest walls in the Dales; monastic
records reveal that during the 13th century it was
increasingly a common practice on estates to
enclose small fields by stone walls, primarily to
exclude other animals.

By the end of the 15th century feudal power had
declined, although Middleham Castle was still in
royal hands, Bolton Castle belonged to the
Scropes, and Skipton Castle to the Cliffords.
Threats from beyond the Scottish Border were
still sufficiently real to merit the building of
fortified houses – Nappa Hall in Wensleydale,
Walburn Hall near Leyburn, and Barden Tower

Fountains Abbey, near Ripon

in Wharfedale, all of 15th-century date. The
Dissolution of the Monasteries, 1537–40, saw the
end of monastic ownership in the Dales; abbeys
and priories became local quarries for good
building stone, but it was not until about 1600 that
the period of farmhouse building really started in
the Dales. Although a few farmhouses and
yeomen's houses date from the decades before the
Civil War the greatest wave of rebuilding occurred
between 1670 and 1700, with a second phase from
1720–50, this one coinciding with a Georgian
improvement to existing houses.

Local stone – preferably sandstone – was used
exclusively. Some buildings, especially in the
lower Dales and around Bolton Abbey in
Wharfedale, have been found still to retain their
cruck-framed timbers, hidden behind stone
exteriors. But throughout the Dales the unity of
building-stones and styles has produced a rare
harmony between buildings and their
environment. Farmhouses, traditional barns,
smaller houses and cottages look right in the
landscape; they have, indeed, grown from it.

Generally speaking buildings are functional
rather than fanciful; local prosperity was never
great enough to merit unnecessary ostentation.
The traditional 17th-century house showed a
long, rectangular plan, two or three bays wide, but
only one room deep, with a front entrance and
sometimes an attached barn or shippon
emphasising the horizontal lines. Offshuts at the
rear were often later additions. From about 1720
the Georgian style infiltrated the Dales, possibly
through the influence of Fountain Hospital at
Linton; houses were higher, squarer, with a
central doorway, vertical sash windows, and using
good masonry mouldings. This style persisted,
with modifications, until Victorian times, by when
large numbers of small, humble cottages had been
added to the village scene to house the lead-
miners, quarrymen, millworkers and artisans who
laboured in small local industries. But local stone
continued to be used, and the low pitch (30
degrees) of stone-slate roofs still echoed the
slopes of background hills.

Above: Haytiming in Littondale
Left: Farming methods in the 1940s

Land management

Between about 1760 and 1840, with a concentration of 20 years each side of 1800, most valley land and the lower hillsides were enclosed by stone walls, hundreds of miles of them. This was done mainly to manage the land more efficiently, control stock-breeding, and improve crop-yields. Barns were built or rebuilt. Shelter-belts and small woodlands were planted. New roads and lanes were aligned between newly-enclosed fields. Thus, today's landscape pattern is largely one of late 18th- and early 19th-century creation – a thousand years later than the settlement pattern. The two illustrate the effect of countless generations of cultural humus laid upon a landscape of superb natural beauty. Recent man-made additions of coniferous woodlands, reservoirs (mainly above Nidderdale), together with the growing scars of limestone quarrying in Ribblesdale, Wharfedale, and lower Wensleydale, have less deleterious effects on the landscape than the disfiguring, disproportionate but permitted structures of new, large agricultural buildings which are outside the planning control of the National Park Committee.

The basic objectives of the National Park Committee, designated in 1954, can conveniently be summarised:

1. To see that the landscape evolves without losing its natural beauty.
2. To enhance the landscape.
3. To give full consideration to local interests.
4. To promote better understanding between town and country.
5. To enable visitors to enjoy the natural beauty.
6. To ensure that recreational activities are compatible and do not harm the natural beauty.

Generally, conservation has priority over recreation. At the same time the needs of agriculture have to be balanced against the claims of conservation. Upland farming depends heavily on public subsidies and before capital grants are paid to farmers for land improvements they are expected to consult the National Park Committee to show that regard has been taken concerning implications for conservation and public enjoyment.

The National Park Committee now offers a wide service with free advice and financial assistance towards certain types of forestry, especially to encourage farmers and landowners to plant locally native or traditional trees, and for management of existing broadleaved amenity woodlands. Grants are also available to cover the cost of repairing boundaries to woods, providing new fencing, to buy and plant trees, and to control rabbits.

But so far as the visiting public are concerned the likeliest impact made by the National Park Committee is through its Information Centres and Warden service. A separate contribution details the Centres (see page 59); six full-time Wardens, many field-workers, and a large number of volunteer helpers work throughout the year to maintain 1000 miles of public footpaths and bridleways, waymarking wherever possible, repairing stiles and footbridges, and supervising an agreed programme of conservation projects, in which almost all the work is done by volunteer groups. All of this represents hundreds of man-hours directed towards the dual aims of conservation and public enjoyment, yet bearing in mind at all times that the area is the work-place for thousands of people who live there. For them, and the countless visitors who are welcomed, the Yorkshire Dales is a particular paradise.

Limestone Scenery

Long scars of bare white rock are the unmistakable mark of limestone stamped on the landscape of the Yorkshire Dales. More than any other rock, limestone imposes its own character on the scenery – with its scars, crags, gorges, sinkholes and caves. It is these features which create such a trademark for the Yorkshire Dales, particularly in the southern part of the Park, where the Great Scar Limestone dominates the country around Malham and Ingleborough, creating what is known as a karst landscape.

Tropical sea
It was therefore a lucky break within the geological record that, 330 million years ago, the Western Yorkshire area was a shallow tropical sea. The ancient slates of that sea floor can be seen beneath the Great Scar Limestone in Ribblesdale, or half way down the Thornton Force waterfall at Ingleton. But it was in the sea that millions of animals lived and died, leaving their broken shells to build up the limestone layers. The Great Scar Limestone was solidified when it was buried beneath a sequence of sandstones, limestones and shales which were deposited by muddy rivers draining into the ancient sea. These became the Yoredale Series of rocks, now forming the summit plinths of the Three Peaks (Ingleborough, Pen-y-ghent and Whernside), and into which are also carved all the northern Dales – they were christened with the ancient name for Wensleydale. The thin Yoredale limestones can hardly dominate the landscape, but they form the caprocks at many of the waterfalls and also define the valley side rock terraces, both of which characterise the northern Dales.

Fractured rock
Massive earth movements later folded and fractured all the rocks and also uplifted them to form the core of the Pennines. The movements created the joints, so conspicuous on any of the limestone plateaux, and displaced the rocks on some massive faults. Giggleswick Scar lies on the

Kilnsey Crag, an unspoilt limestone cliff

most obvious of the famous Craven Faults; the fault line is traced by the A65 road west of Settle, where limestone crags rise high on the north side but the same rock lies buried deep beneath younger sandstones just across the road. The fractures also provided pathways for hot fluids migrating through the rock when it was deeply buried; these deposited the minerals of lead, zinc and barium which miners have since torn from the long thin veins in the limestone, notably beneath Grassington Moor and the Swaledale area.

The carving of the landscape
A much later stage in the geological history of the Yorkshire Dales was the carving of the landscape, mostly by rivers and glaciers within the last million years or so. At times, ice covered the entire Dales area – it was probably a kilometre thick in places – but the ice sheets expanded and waned a number of times in response to the climatic changes. Hills and valleys were moulded successively by rivers and glaciers, but a vital aspect of the erosion was when glaciers flowed in the confines of the valleys, opening them out to create the broad floors and steep sides which so characterise the Dales.

The broad features of the landscape were very much fashioned by the glaciers, but the character of the limestone dominates the details of the scenery. Along the flanks of many of the Dales, the limestone beds stand proud as long lines of bare white crags and scars. Twistleton Scars and Raven Scar along opposite sides of Chapel-le-Dale are among the finest. Their rock faces were plucked clean by the passing glaciers and have survived since the end of the Ice Age due firstly to the strength of the limestone and secondly to its complete solution in rainwater so that no debris remains to form a soil. Most of the scars clearly relate to the limestone bedding but some are on a larger scale. Just south of the confluence of the Wharfedale and Littondale glaciers, a rock spur was trimmed right back to form Kilnsey Crag, a spectacular overhanging limestone face.

Limestone pavements
High above the staircase of scars, the glaciers once also overrode the broad plateaux, and there the combination of ice and limestone has excelled. The limestone pavements of Yorkshire are unforgettable. During the last Ice Age, 15,000 years ago, glaciers scoured the limestone clean, and since then rainwater has slowly eaten into the rock. It has cut little solution runnels across the slabs, and has opened the fractures into wide rounded rifts; these are known as grikes, and the blocks between are called clints. On the famous pavement at the top of Malham Cove, the numerous runnels and grikes create a highly dissected surface, in total contrast to the pavements of north-western Ingleborough which have much broader clints with widely spaced runnels. Even more impressive is the southern spur of Whernside, Scales Moor, where huge expanses of pavement are devoid of vegetation.

The effects of rainwater
The solutional features of the pavements exist because the limestone is dissolved by rainwater, though of course extremely slowly. The same process permits underground drainage of the

The precipitous face of Malham Cove (right)

karst country. Water gets into the narrow joints of any rock, but moves so slowly that it can only enlarge the fractures by chemical solution. Limestone is therefore the only common rock where fractures are opened up, eventually to become caves, on a scale adequate to absorb all surface drainage. So a characteristic of the limestone hills is the vast number of sinkholes – which may be anything from tiny fissures taking just seepage water, to gaping holes swallowing large streams. Particularly common in the Dales are shakeholes – conical depressions 2–20m across which pockmark the sheets of glacial boulder clay overlying the limestone. They have formed as the sediment has been washed down into the open limestone fissures below: analogies with an egg-timer are most appropriate. There are thousands of them in the Dales, and perhaps those on the southern slopes of Ingleborough are among the finest.

Caves and potholes
Streams commonly sink into larger openings – potholes if they are vertical shafts or caves if they are closer to horizontal. These are some of the highlights of the Dales landscapes. Most famous is Gaping Gill, high on south-eastern Ingleborough, where Fell Beck plummets into darkness, falling 110m down a shaft 10m across which opens into a massive chamber down below. A more impressive view from the surface is provided by Alum Pot, on the north-eastern slopes of Ingleborough. It is a huge rift in the hillside, long enough and wide enough to see right down past the rock ledges to the floor 60m below. Today little water flows down it, as the larger stream which formed the pothole now sinks further back up the hill where it has found a new underground route.

The Butter Tubs
A group of potholes called the Butter Tubs are well known because of their roadside location on the pass from Wensleydale to Swaledale north of Hawes. Unlike the bold rift of Alum Pot, they are irregular shaped shafts fluted where their walls have been cut back by small streams draining from the nearby peat haggs. Only 20m deep, they cut almost the full thickness of a thin Yoredale limestone. Between these extremes of size and shape, there are hundreds of potholes on the high slopes of the Yorkshire hills – each carved by its own stream, each different, and each unique to limestone.

Cave streams
All the water that sinks into the limestone eventually has to return to daylight. Collecting underground into a series of larger cave streams, most of it emerges from just a handful of risings; in the Three Peaks area there are one or two in the floor of each main valley. The water may pour from an open cave mouth, such as Clapham Beck Head where the Gaping Gill water rediscovers the open air on the south side of Ingleborough. Alternatively the rising may be a dark, still pool, like Keld Head just below the road in Kingsdale, where a powerful river rises silently from a submerged cave.

Between the sinkholes and the risings lie the caves – the underground arteries which have captured the natural drainage. They all started life as narrow fissures in the limestone, but the flow of

Top: Entering Rumbling Hole, Leck Fell
Bottom: The effects of water erosion

water over tens of thousands of years has enlarged them into wide open tunnels. The simplest form of cave is a single streamway with long stretches of gently descending passage interrupted by vertical shafts where a joint has guided the water down to greater depths. Gaping Gill is the prime example of a shaft, though on an uncharacteristically large scale, and the passage in the White Scar show cave, at Ingleton, is a typical active streamway. A single stream cascades into Calf Holes, beside the Pennine Way above Ribblesdale, and emerges from Browgill Cave just 500m away. This is a complete cave system in miniature, but even smaller is God's Bridge further down the same stream, where the water ducks underground for just ten metres, finding a bedding plane which it follows back to the hillside.

Underground mazes
Most caves are much more complex. Perhaps a dozen sinking streams may unite underground in a single cave river, to create a rambling, branching system. Yet more complication is added by the dimension of depth. Water always tries to find the lowest route through the limestone, and over time it progressively abandons passages at higher

levels. The tourist section of Ingleborough Cave is a tunnel once used by the Gaping Gill drainage, but it is now almost dry as today's water flows in a younger parallel stream cave at a lower level. Where a series of tributary stream caves cut down through a host of old abandoned tunnels, the result can be a gigantic three dimensional maze. Under the western edge of the limestone, north of Ingleton, the Ease Gill Cave System has nearly 50km of interconnected passages of all sorts and sizes. There are narrow twisting fissures, and sweeping tunnels 15m high and wide; there are huge silent caverns, and roaring waterfall shafts; and there are beautiful displays of stalactites and stalagmites where dripwater has redeposited some of the dissolved limestone as sparkling white calcite.

Because the drainage is underground, much of the surface maybe dry; even major valleys can be streamless. Kingsdale was largely cut by Ice Age glaciers, but the modern stream bypasses it through a long cave system under its western flank. Only in flood does the main beck carry too much water to be absorbed by the debris-choked sinkholes at the edge of the limestone; then the channel (artificially straightened) down the floor of Kingsdale carries a short-lived torrent of floodwater. Upper Littondale also has a cave route which in dry weather can take all the drainage; it leaves a streambed of dry rock through Litton village.

Effects of the Ice Age
A permanently dry valley extends from Gaping Gill down through the gorge of Trow Gill into the upper end of Clapdale. Its size and shape tell that it is not of glacial origin but was cut by a small river. During the Ice Ages there were times when there was no immediate ice cover, but the ground was deep frozen and the existing caves were blocked by ice. Meltwater from snowfields and nearby glaciers therefore flowed on the surface of the limestone, and cut the valley, deepening into a gorge on the steeper gradient down through Trow

A field study party examines the limestone pavement at Ingleborough

Gill. Since the climate has improved, the limestone has lost its seal of ice, the drainage has returned underground, and the valley has been left dry.

Meltwater streams
These meltwater streams were largely responsible for cutting so many of the dry valleys and gorges in the Dales limestone country. The most spectacular results are found at Malham. Fed from dying ice on the Malham Tarn upland, two major meltwater rivers flowed south, and cascaded off the edge of the limestone plateau along the fault line through Malham village. The western river cut the splendid Watlowes valley, now dry, and at the edge of the plateau dropped over a massive waterfall which cut back to form a vertical face in the limestone. That is at least part of the story behind the dramatic 70m high cliff of Malham Cove, though the great width of the Cove suggests that ice may also have played a role in a rather more complex history. Two kilometres to the east, the second river cut the Gordale valley. At the edge of the plateau it did not form a single waterfall, but instead used the steeper gradient and a series of cascades to incise itself into a narrow gorge. Gordale Scar is a monumental feature with its cliffs towering 100m above the shadowy depths; within it a natural arch is a remnant of cave passage revealed when the gorge cut down into it. The stream through Gordale today is tiny compared to the torrent which must have cut the gorge, and now that most of the water is underground the cliffs stand uneroded as a reminder of those bygone events.

The Gordale cliffs and the Scales Moor pavements may have been cut by water and ice, but both only exist because the rock is limestone. The same applies to the potholes and caves, and they have all combined to develop the unmistakable character of the Yorkshire Dales landscape.

A Day in the Life of a Dalesman

Clark Stones has spent most of his life as a farmer in the Upper Dales. Conditions are often testing and sometimes cruel

Daybreak

Arkengarthdale – 'Ark'nd'l' to the natives – daybreak, early April. . . . As he fought off lingering sleep farmer Clark Stones was aware that the long winter sequence of silent dawns was now interrupted by a symphony of sounds – blackbirds staking territorial claims, lapwings piping impertinent wolf-whistles, curlews bubbling in composed jubilation – the avian prelude to summer. Nevertheless last night's cloudless skies and still dank air had warned him of a hard frost to threaten any lamb improvidently born of darkness on the hillsides.

His thoughts floated back to the evening's final rounds and the pathetic near-strangled lamb he had delivered from a neighbour's exhausted ewe. It was lucky he had been able to manipulate its legs and wrest it from its fateful predicament – head out, but one foreleg crooked preventing its dropping. He had taken it down with its dam to a protective straw-filled barn, but he knew by its bloated discoloured face that its chances were slim. At such times care and compassion over-rule all other considerations.

In the short space it takes to tumble into clothes and gulp a hasty cup of tea, he was back in the fields right up to the moor's edge, searching every wall corner or hidden gully for ewes in difficult labour or lambs in need of assistance. Throughout, his practised eye subconsciously scanned the containing drystone walls for gaps that might tempt the inquisitive ewes to stray.

Like his father and grandfather who farmed before him, Clark Stones was born and bred in the dale. From the village school he earned a grammar school place at Richmond where, because of Arkengarthdale's remoteness, he had to be a boarder. A natural athlete, he played an active part in all sports, laying the foundations for future satisfaction and success in the field, particularly in cricket and rugby.

After university in Scotland, two years' National Service with the Royal Engineers allowed further indulgence of his sporting inclinations, highlighted when he refused selection for a commission to spend three months with his regiment on intensive ski-training in Germany. A year with the Forestry Commission in Argyllshire allowed a continuance of his favourite sports, cricket, rugby and ski-ing, extended at this time to include water-ski-ing on the sea lochs. He later resigned to join his father and learn the craft of farming at Pepper Hall Farm in Arkengarthdale. By the time he was thirty the farm was made over to him, although his father continued to assist in semi-retirement for another twelve years.

Married to an equally active, sporting and hard-working wife, Greta, he has two teenage sons. Robert, the eldest, works on a nearby farm and follows a day-release course in agriculture at a local college. Later he hopes to spend a couple of years in the United States, after which the farm will be open, if he wishes, to ease him into ownership. Philip, the youngest, boards at Barnard Castle School. His future is deliberately undetermined. Like their parents, the boys are enthusiastic skiers, both of a calibre approaching international standard. They also share an enthusiasm for motor-cycle scrambling, the rugged terrain of much of the home farm being ideally suited for its pursuit.

Clark hung up his rugby boots a few years ago after considerable service to Darlington Rugby Union Football Club. His cricketing interests, apart from a rare deputising appearance on the field, concentrate now on the chairmanship of Reeth Cricket Club. But the family addiction to ski-ing persists, often to the extent of precipitating a hard 250 mile overnight drive to Glenshee to participate in downhill races, followed by an immediate exhausted return to the ever demanding livestock.

His early round of the sheep completed, Clark's attention had now to be concentrated on the cattle, especially the milkers. The Dairy Crest's blue and white tanker would call at 10.30 am, by which time not only had 17 cows to be milked, but the milk had to be cooled to below 40F before it could be taken.

Nine cows were led into the milking parlour, haltered, and given water and food to settle them. Immaculate in long white coat, Clark sensitively washed down each cow before attaching its individual milker. The cows appeared to enjoy the experience, while the farm cats looked on in anticipation of their share. Farm cats are maintained principally to keep down vermin. Since they hunt for pleasure, not for food, and the healthiest make the best hunters, their ration is neither grudged nor stinted.

The nine having been milked and the milk decanted into the cooler in the nearby dairy, silage had to be led by tractor from the outside clamp to circular feeding stalls. The milked cows were put to them to feed while the remaining eight milkers were brought into the parlour from their loose housing for a repeat performance.

Mid morning

Having already accomplished the equivalent of a townsman's half-day's work, it was now time for a hearty traditional breakfast, a chance to skim the contents of the ominous buff envelopes brought by the postman, and the opportunity to update Greta on the lambing situation. After all, she might at any time be called upon to take in to nurse and feed some weakling lamb or one rejected by its mother. In any case, on a one-man farm, it is only prudent that the farmer's wife is fully acquainted with all aspects of its operation in the dreaded event of an unforeseen emergency.

No time to linger after breakfast. A bucketful of concentrates fed to the breeding ewes in an in-bye meadow offered the opportunity for a precautionary inspection of those immediately due to drop their lambs. Their unaccustomed trot to their feed flushed a startled snipe into typical zig-zag flight, while a flash of white along the wall top betrayed the season's first wheatear, newly arrived from far off tropical Africa.

Near the congregated ewes Clark noticed a wet patch – probably a fractured field drain – and made a mental note to investigate further in less pressured times. There were other peaty patches in the steeply sloping field, some badly poached by heavy-footed cattle in last year's damp late autumn. But there was also a broad dark trampled swath angled down the field to a corner near the village – the tell-tale legacy of a party of fifty schoolchildren and their transgressing teachers – only a stone's throw from a public right of way along a dry metalled track! With only fifty-five acres of harvestable grass for essential winter fodder and the prohibitive cost of bought-in substitutes, such damage could, in hard times, have critical consequences. Our Dalesman reflected on the deed with philosophical calm when others might, with cause, have been roused to angry protestation.

Feeding the ewes and young lambs

Back at the big barn the black and white Friesian bull and some fifty young or in-calf followers were beginning to voice a peevish demand for food and attention. Hay and concentrates were issued in measured quantities, straw was laid, and a considerate, educated eye measured their health and appearance, each and every one a distinctive individual.

The rumble of the milk tanker drew Clark to assist at the dairy. Drivers are in such a continual hurry to meet manufacturing deadlines at the dairy in Northallerton that any assistance is welcomed. The produce of each herd is regularly examined for milk-fat and bacteriological content, demanding close attention to hygiene and diet. The consequences of electrical breakdown hindering the cooling process, or of roads impassable through snowstorm or flash flood preventing collection might plague uneasier minds, but lifelong experience with the animals and the elements induces in the Dales farmer a patience and inner calm greatly to be envied.

Midday

The next task was the inescapable mucking out of the milking parlour by the traditional shovel and barrow, followed by scraping out the loose house by tractor, the manure being deposited directly into the muck spreader. Fresh straw was then spread, and the stock brought in again. The barley straw is brought from a lowland farm at Eppleby, some twenty miles distant to the north-east, coincidentally the object of the next assignment.

The unpredictable climate of the dale, the inhospitable altitude of the farm straddling the 1000 foot contour, and the uncompromising nature of the land – steep, peaty, and pocked with lead-impregnated debris from former lead mining – preclude the over-wintering of the whole flock at Pepper Hall Farm. So for five winter months each year the hoggs (last year's lambs) are taken to kinder pastures. A former school-fellow and rugby team-mate who farms at Eppleby acts as host to about fifty hoggs, mostly gimmers (females), as well as providing the bedding straw. Yesterday Clark drove over to collect half of them. Now he could bring back the remainder.

The family's devotion to ski-ing had dictated the rejection of the ubiquitous Land Rover in favour of an estate car in which the children could sleep on the long journeys to and from the Scottish ski slopes. The trailer was securely attached and Fly, the oldest and most reliable of the four sheep dogs, leapt willingly inside. Down the track to the old mining village of Langthwaite, up past the CB Inn, Clark turned right on to the historic Stang road – used certainly in Roman times, and probably for centuries before.

The steep one-in-four ascent invoked recollection of desperate experience with tractor and straw-loaded trailer travelling downhill. The risk of a tractor running out of control on the steep hillsides of the dale is always in the minds of the farmers, many of whom have been fortunate to survive overturning or collision. Broad bands of uprooted conifers in the Stang Forest offered stark reminders of the severe gales that rattled the area in January leaving a wake of fallen trees, broken walls, and perforated roofs. The A66 – the Roman 'Street' across Stainmore – was beginning to feel the weight of the early visitor.

The hoggs, gently driven into the trailer at Eppleby, had a healthy, well-fed appearance. One wether (male) hogg had died, and a gimmer had ripped off an entangled horn, but otherwise their stay had brought great benefit. The return journey, through Richmond to avoid the dreaded descent of the Stang with such a heavy load, was taken at a cautious speed.

Back at the farm they were unloaded and driven into a disused farm building along with yesterday's batch, to await drenching and marking before release on to the moor.

Clark had now put in the equivalent of many a townsman's full working day, and it was time to pause for a well-earned lunch.

The fifty hoggs were penned in the large doorless kitchen of the old Low Lockhouse Farm (datestone 1781), several adopting strategic stances on the raised central hearth or the flanking upper recesses below an embracing three-arched chimney breast. All pure Swaledales, the majority were gimmer hoggs. Towards the end of the year the weakest would be sold off at Hawes Auction Mart, leaving the healthiest forty to maintain the flock's breeding stock. They now had to be prepared for the moor.

Clark inspects the horns of each tup

Each in turn was captured and, firmly grasped between the farmer's knees, dosed through the mouth with a potion to eradicate flukes and other internal infections. There followed a careful inspection of each animal, revealing in two cases horns growing into the flesh just below the eyes. These had to be carefully pruned with a hacksaw. All were stripe-marked with rud (red dye) over the shoulders – the farm's distinctive livery.

Drenching and marking accomplished, the hoggs were driven by the dogs up through the fields to the moor wall. Once through the gate they were left to pick their individual ways to their traditional 'heafs'. These are the parts of the moor where generation after generation of whole families of sheep have assumed almost exclusive grazing territories to which they always return after removal or dispersal. This ancient system of moorland sheep management is helpful because they learn the locations of the choicest grazing patches and sheltered hollows, but also build up immunity to indigenous infestations. Additionally, and of crucial importance on this particular piece of open moorland, they have learnt to avoid the fatal vegetation of the lead spoil heaps that in recent times have claimed the lives of three heifers (young cows).

Here, dark mysterious tunnels, some miles in length, drain subterranean water from old lead workings and untold caves; strange ruins and mountains of mine waste create fantastic landscapes; while more recent quarrying of dark grey marble-like chert has left vast carpets of scree-like debris to deface the heathery hillsides. All seem havens for the resurgent rabbits that mercifully for the farmers' sake have been dramatically culled by a long cold winter.

The tractor is used for a variety of tasks

From the fellside Clark returned through the pastures to check again on the lambing ewes, to supplement their diet with hay and concentrates, and to reassure himself on their well-being. On the banks of a gurgling beck the first gold coltsfoot flashed a friendly greeting, while in the water the lush watercress and the spreading brooklime promised an early splash of colour. The customary herons were not to be seen. Perhaps they had started to build their nests.

The hazy sun was beginning to sink towards the high hilly horizons, but there was still much that needed attention. The morning's routine of milking, fothering, mucking out and strawing was all to be repeated, as it was on the other 364 days a year. Young calves in outlying byres demanded food and water. Last night's half-strangled lamb had to be checked – it was now miraculously none the worse for its unhappy entrance into the world. And a score of other minor chores could be put off no longer.

Clark checks the udders of a cow that has recently dropped its calf

Dusk

High tea afforded a relaxing interlude, but with Robert now back from his daily employment, there was still an hour or so of daylight for him to help his father rebuild a section of fallen wall. Once damaged, early repair is essential not only to retain the sheep, but also to prevent great lengths falling like toppling dominoes. For though they may not be as old as the hills, many extend back over several centuries, and with care will last as long again.

Repairing a section of drystone wall

Their mortarless construction follows the age-old principle of a firm broad footing (foundation) and two converging walls erected in overlapping courses, the centre packed with small stones, tied intermediately with 'troughs' (through or tie stones spanning the full width of the wall and sometimes extruding at the faces), built up to about five feet then finished with top stones or cap stones, often set on end for extra stability. The stones of clumsily irregular shapes and sizes require skilful selection and placement, making what may appear to be a fairly simple and straightforward process a matter of real craftsmanship, if not a true art form. The walls are as much an integral part of landscape and heritage as man himself, with his animals the architect and preserver of the present scenario.

The walling gave Clark and Robert a chance to discuss their days' transactions and the conditions of the livestock, until too soon they realised that encroaching darkness obliged a final round of the fields with the breeding ewes.

Evening

Their torchlight return to the farmhouse, to collapse into comfortable armchairs to contemplate the state of the farm, or at the insistence of the inevitable television the state of the nation, was not necessarily the end of the working day. With a family of over 200 animals, who knew what calls or crises might suddenly be thrust upon them, even in the still, small hours?

Justifiably, after some fifteen hours of hard manual outdoor work and the ever-present weight of all his responsibilities, Clark decided to put off once again those unending returns for the nine-to-five men from the ministry and the Inland Revenue. Perhaps half an hour on the piano and a few choruses from Mendelssohn's *Elijah* might be more conducive to a quiet night.

Arkil, after whose garth (enclosure) the dale is named, was the son of Gospatric the Viking pre-conquest landowner. When the Conqueror made over the estates to Alan, Earl of Richmond, it was significant that he appointed the same Robert Arkil his head forester. One is tempted to consider whether Arkil's position was changed in any way, and if he did not continue in his original position of influence and social standing. His modest dignity, his strength and resilience, his inspiration of trust and a courteous refusal to scrape to usurped authority, are qualities that have been passed down and preserved in modern times in the character of the authentic Dalesman.

Clark Stones is a man of such qualities, graced to be, as Shelley wrote of Hunt, 'one of those happy souls which are the salt of the earth'. In hands like these, with pride and concern for the heritage he has become part of, the nation can rest assured that at least the little part of England that falls within his stewardship will be lovingly preserved.

In a rare quiet moment Clark finds time to survey the beauty of his surroundings

Recreation in the Dales

The hills and dales of north-west Yorkshire make a magnificent backdrop for recreation, whether to the athlete bent on strenuous physical exertion, or to the gently strolling country-lover.

A thousand-plus miles of well-defined public paths and ancient tracks beside sparkling streams and waterfalls, through meadows dotted with wild flowers and fragrant upland pastures, or even on the wildest hagg-pocked moorlands evoke feelings of tranquillity not often achieved in 20th-century life.

Pathfinding

Many visitors to the Dales, conscious that most of the land is privately owned, are anxious about trespass and interference with and by livestock. Respect for other people's property and privacy is right and proper, but this must not inhibit your rightful enjoyment of the countryside which warmhearted Dalesfolk, proud of their heritage, are pleased to share with you.

Throughout the area is a comprehensive network of public footpaths indicated by fingerposts and symbols, if not by visible evidence on the ground. Footpaths are further identified by yellow discs or arrows on gateposts and stiles, and on walls or buildings where there is a possibility of going astray. Bridleways, identified by larger blue discs or patches, are open to pedestrians, but also to horse riders and cyclists.

Using Ordnance Survey maps

All these paths and bridleways, as well as roads used as public paths, are indicated in red on the maps in this book, and on all the other *Landranger* maps of the Ordnance Survey. They are shown by broken green lines on the 1 : 25000 *Outdoor Leisure* maps and on the 1 : 25000 *Pathfinder* series, which also include for additional definition all field boundaries and further details of local features and facilities. These three Ordnance Survey map series help not only to find one's way around but, because of all the information they display, simplify holiday planning without the fear of overlooking places and features of special interest.

Guided walks

For many visitors the most rewarding introduction to the area will be through the National Park's comprehensive programme of guided walks led by local people with intimate knowledge and infinite enthusiasm for the countryside in which they live.

These gentle afternoon walks averaging three to four miles in distance and up to three hours in duration are well within the capabilities of most people. They usually have a central theme such as flowers, birds, farming, local history, geology and lead mining, but embrace consideration of the whole environment. Of particular interest to children, a number of farm visits and sheep dog demonstrations are made along the way.

Birdwatching at Malham Tarn

Details of the walks are available at the National Park Information Centres or in *The Visitor*, the National Park's free newspaper that also contains articles about the heritage and traditions of the Yorkshire Dales and the people who live and work in them.

'Dales Rail' guided walks
Those whose holidays encompass the first weekend of every month from May to October will have the unique opportunity of combining a ride along the country's most spectacular railway – the controversial Settle–Carlisle line – with the choice of up to a dozen free guided walks from an easy six miles to a strenuous twenty. The 'Dales Rail' service, set up in 1975 under the joint organisation of the Yorkshire Dales National Park, the West Yorkshire Passenger Transport Executive and British Rail, offers to people from West Yorkshire, Lancashire and North Cumbria, access to the Dales and opportunities for countryside recreation otherwise denied since the closure of the line to local traffic in 1970.

Details of the walks and the times of trains and connecting buses are available from the Yorkshire Dales National Park, Bainbridge, Leyburn, North Yorkshire. Dales people and visitors may also use the service for day outings to Carlisle, Leeds and Bradford.

Self-guided walks
For those who find map-reading a mystery or a distraction several options present themselves. The simplest is a series of well-defined walks or nature trails, some of which are on private land (necessitating the payment of a small entrance fee). They include Hardraw Force in Wensleydale, The Malham Tarn Nature Trail, The Reginald Farrer Nature Trail from Clapham, and the Ingleton Waterfalls Trail. Most have descriptive leaflets, some of which are published by the National Park. This book includes 16 easy-to-follow, circular walks specially geared to family groups who want to spend a day or so exploring the Dales at their own pace. In addition the National Park also publishes an increasing range of low-cost self-guided walk leaflets that explain simply and clearly the directions to be taken, and indicate and interpret points of interest to look out for. These are available at any of the National Park Centres.

Famous footpaths
The Dales Way – from Ilkley to Bowness – is classified as a 'Recreational Path' by the Countryside Commission. To cross the northern dales A Wainwright's *A Coast to Coast Walk* is popular and the prestigious Pennine Way, which is a designated 'Long Distance Footpath' is described in detail on pages 26–30.

The Three Peaks
The ultimate challenge for walkers in the Yorkshire Dales is the demanding 22-mile switchback plod over the summits of Pen-y-ghent, Whernside and Ingleborough. Its completion within twelve hours (average eight hours) qualifies for membership of The Three Peaks of Yorkshire Club based at Pen-y-ghent Café, Horton in Ribblesdale, Settle, North Yorkshire. The walk is detailed in *Walks in the Limestone Country* by A Wainwright, *Yorkshire's Three Peaks* by The Dalesman, and *The Three Peaks Map and Guide* by

Crossing the finishing line of the Mountain Marathon, Howgill Fells

Stiles Publications. Potential walkers should be warned that severely adverse weather and underfoot conditions can combine at short notice to make this a punishing endurance or even survival test.

Visitors should recognise that many public footpaths cross pastures and meadows whose crops are critical to the whole agricultural economy. Within the Yorkshire Dales where soils, altitude and climate militate against arable farming, the total emphasis is on grass production. The grass, whether as permanent year-round sustenance or in hay and silage as vital winter feed, is used to build up sturdy young sheep and cattle to be fattened for the table on lowland farms, or to sustain the dairy products for which the Dales are so famous. Isaiah said 'All flesh is grass', but here in the Dales one could equally say 'All grass is flesh'.

It is therefore not only courteous but also provident to keep crop damage to the minimum by walking in single file across enclosed pastures.

Livestock
The law now permits farmers to graze certain breeds of beef bulls with cows or heifers in fields crossed by public footpaths. Provided they are not provoked and given a wide berth, these animals will regard you with nothing more than curiosity. It cannot be over stressed, however, that all animals should be treated with respect, but the solitary black and white dairy bull should be avoided at all costs. After calving, some cows can become aggressive if you place yourself between them and their calf.

All animals, including humans, are naturally curious, and so you can expect your gazes to be reciprocated. But they are also easily excited, and therefore dogs should be kept on leads at all times, and restrained from provoking livestock by barking or lunging at them. This is equally important with sheep and lambs, and it is well to remember that if chased, pregnant cows and sheep can easily miscarry.

Farmers complain with justification about the problems created by the occasional careless visitor failing to secure gates after them. The mixing of different farmers' stock, disruption of cropping regimes, premature or unwanted mating, spread of infection, straying on to highways with consequent danger both to traffic and to the animals: these are just a few of the possible consequences of a momentary lapse of concentration or consideration. So please, fasten all gates securely behind you.

A group of potholers discuss tactics at the mouth of Ingleborough Cave

Caves and potholes

From Nidderdale in the east to Barbondale in the west no less than 200km of natural underground drainage channels have been explored and surveyed. With many more awaiting discovery, the area can justifiably be called 'The Cave District'.

To some, the words caves and potholes conjure up thoughts of dangerous places fit only for savage beasts or malevolent spirits. To others they represent mystery and wonder, challenge and adventure, their exploration a source of excitement.

The sport of caving or potholing calls upon advanced skills. Physically very demanding and beset with potential dangers like unexpected shafts, rockfalls and sudden flooding, it is one to be contemplated only under expert tuition. But in the Yorkshire Dales the curious and adventurous can meet their aspirations by a simple progression.

Show caves

Within the National Park are three show caves where visitors are given conducted tours along comfortable illuminated passages. The White Scar Cave at Ingleton with its stream, its spectacular waterfalls, its stalactites and stalagmites and displaying clearly the geological unconformity of the district, makes an interesting appetiser, even for the disabled in wheelchairs.

Stump Cross Caverns at Greenhow Hill between Grassington and Pateley Bridge extends the experience by the inclusion of two new dimensions: its one-time occupation by wolverine, bison, fox and reindeer proved by the finds of fossilised bones; and the intrusive workings of centuries of lead miners. Stump Cross guides complete their tours with a compelling colour video film by Sid Perou on the inner recesses of the caverns and the caving techniques used to explore them. Both White Scar and Stump Cross offer free parking and restaurant facilities.

Ingleborough Cave is a pleasant mile and a half walk up Clapdale from the Clapham National Park Centre and car park. Arguably the most natural of the show caves it features stalactites, stalagmites, the active growth of tufa, and other interesting geological features including large fossils in the cave walls. Of particular interest to many are the albino shrimps, worms and insect larvae in the stream and pools. Recently, the long-anticipated breakthrough has been made between this system and that of Gaping Gill, a mile further up the dale.

An intrepid potholer descends into the abyss

Gaping Gill

Gaping Gill is the country's most spectacular pothole falling sheerly from an awesome oval 'gape' 20m by 10m across down to Britain's largest chamber – about the size of York Minster – some 104m below. Impressive from above, the chamber is breathtaking from below with water cascading all the way down to sink mysteriously into the floor to follow deeper explored passages that emerge in Ingleborough Cave. For the ten days preceding Spring and August Bank Holidays the Craven and Bradford Pothole Clubs erect a winch at the mouth to permit the public to descend and share in its wonders.

For the walker a range of caves of reasonable access and safety exist throughout the area, of which the most popular are the historic Victoria and Attermire Caves, approached from Settle or Langcliffe, and Yorda's Cave in Kingsdale. Accounts of such caves and how to approach them are found in A Wainwright's *Walks in Limestone Country* and his *Walks in the Howgill Fells*.

Caving instruction

The Whernside National Caving Training Centre, operated by the Yorkshire Dales National Park, mounts a wide range of caving courses throughout the year. One of its most popular offerings is a one-day introductory caving course that features a morning of talks, slide shows and demonstration followed by an afternoon's guided exploration in a cave. Experienced cavers of all grades can select from a wide range of weekend, five-day or one week courses. Fell-walking, natural history, bird-watching, canoeing and multi-activity courses are also available, of which the canoeing and bird-watching courses are offered as one-day options. Full particulars are obtainable from Whernside Cave and Fell Centre, Dent, Sedbergh, Cumbria LA10 5RE, *tel* Dent (05875) 213, location: OS map reference SD 725858.

Mineral and stone mines

Almost since time began man has been mining the Dales for minerals and stone. Lead mining, its most profitable venture, was concentrated in two major fields, from Grassington Moor to Greenhow Hill, and in North Swaledale bestraddling Arkengarthdale. In these areas in particular, extensive evidence of former burrowings and burnings is revealed by tailings (spoil heaps), bell pits, adits and levels (tunnels), watercourses and reservoirs, crushing and smelt mills and tunnel-like flues extending up steep hillsides. Elsewhere shafts of old copper, calamine (zinc) and coal mines, and the tunnels of the Wensleydale slate mines invite the attention of the curious. It must be emphasised that unlike the natural caves and potholes of the limestone areas, these old man-made passages are most unsafe and should not be entered at any cost. Artefacts and implements, rock samples and pictures of their former operation are now well represented in folk museums like Hawes and Grassington, but especially at the Mines Museum at Earby, south of Skipton. Their history is well documented by local authors A Raistrick and R T Clough, and in the journals of the Northern Mine Research Society, South Anston, Sheffield.

Hawes underground stone mine

Cycling

An ideal way to explore the picturesque villages and the ancient wandering lanes of the valleys is by cycle. The leisurely self-dictated pace, the constant opportunity to stop and stare whenever the inclination moves, and the direct impact of the countryside – the sights, the scents and the sounds – combine to generate a sense of well-being and an empathy with one's surroundings.

To reach another dale or some high vantage point may necessitate a bit of uphill pushing, but the subsequent rewards of splendid panoramic views and the exhilarating downhill coast will more than compensate. Cycles may be hired from

Hawes trotting race, where galloping is strictly against the rules

the Ropeworks in Hawes, and from a number of shops in the larger towns.

Pony trekking

Equally rewarding for the less energetic or the lover of animals is to commune with the countryside on the back of a well-schooled Dales pony. Four centres offer one-hour, half-day and full day treks, as well as tuition and longer trails. Details of these are given in the Directory (p68).

Swimming

The Dales abound with becks and streams which can be fun for children to splash around in, though few offer safe pools deep or calm enough for swimming. Exceptions may be found in the lower reaches of the southern sector, as at Bolton Abbey in Wharfedale or Stainforth Force in Ribblesdale, but even these can be dangerous in spate or unhealthy in drought. Council-maintained swimming pools of very high standard exist at Skipton, Settle, Ingleton, Threshfield and Richmond.

Angling

The rivers and becks afford excellent opportunities in their appropriate seasons for trout and grayling fishing. Of particular interest to the disabled is the facility at Widdale Beck near Hawes for wheelchair anglers. However in this area, as well as one or two others, no fishing is allowed on Sundays. Trout fishing is also available at a number of reservoirs, and on a few privately-owned lakes like Malham Tarn and Semer Water, which offer the additional opportunity of catching perch. Fly fishing for rainbow trout is available at Kilnsey Park in Wharfedale. On the southern fringe of the National Park, the Leeds to Liverpool Canal offers the opportunity of coarse fishing to its devotees. Full details of all locations, clubs, riparian owners and conditions, are provided in *The Northern Anglers' Handbook* (Dalesman), available from information centres and newsagents. The Yorkshire Water Authority, whose rod licence must be carried by all anglers, offers a free *Customer's Guide* to all locations.

Canal cruising

Closely linked with the history and economy of the southern parts, the Leeds to Liverpool Canal can offer a different perspective to the Dales and adjacent area, or act as a base for excursions into the National Park. Traditional narrow boats are hired on a weekly basis from Pennine Cruisers, 19 Coach St, Skipton or IML, Bank Newton, Skipton, North Yorkshire.

It is not possible to detail all the activities open to the visitor. Those seeking a new and exciting experience may well be attracted by the hot air balloon flights operated from Grassington. Some may wish to watch the graceful soaring hang gliders concentrated around the scars above Hawes. Some will want to join with the Dalesfolk in their village galas and agricultural shows often featuring fell races and sheep dog trials; in the annual brass band contest at Hardraw or the sulky racing at Hawes; in the snooker, carpet bowls and badminton offered by village institutes; or in the cultural offerings of the Grassington, Settle and Richmond festivals of the arts.

The character and beauty of the Yorkshire Dales has been shaped over countless generations by the people who live in them and their stewardship of their inheritance. Increasing dependence on technological innovation has reduced demand for agricultural labour, setting in motion a process of depopulation often manifested by the closure of village schools and shops, and the decimation of bus and other essential services. Tourism is seen as one possible factor in reversing that process.

Partly for this reason, but principally because they want to share the heritage of which they are so justifiably proud, the people of the Dales offer you a warm welcome and generous hospitality.

Looking down on Littondale

The Pennine Way through the Dales

The 270 miles of the Pennine Way, Britain's first, and arguably finest Long Distance Footpath, hold a special fascination for all ramblers. The Pennine Way is the hillwalkers' Everest without the distance or the dangers, something to be tackled because 'it's there'. If you are young and strong and have three weeks to spare, a pack on your back and are prepared to pit yourself against the worst that the elements can throw at you across the wildest country in Britain, the Pennine Way can be yours.

But lesser mortals can also enjoy the Pennine Way on a less epic scale. You can, of course, confine yourself to a short length, finding pleasant pubs, youth hostels or guesthouses at which to stay. If you have a willing friend with a car you can be dropped off and collected at various points to enjoy the Pennine Way in day stages, and better still, if you are prepared to take just a little trouble with bus and rail timetables, you can complete a good deal of the Way, at least in its southern and central sections, by making use of public transport. The Ramblers' Association produces an excellent Bed and Breakfast Guide which includes many addresses on the Pennine Way, whilst the Pennine Way Council, a national body established to co-ordinate information about the footpath, produces an accommodation guide which also details local transport.

Contrasting scenery

If you are choosing a section to walk as an introduction to the Pennine Way, there is no doubt that the 60 miles or so within the Yorkshire Dales offer the finest range of scenery. This is the Pennine Way at its best, full of contrast, with moments of real drama, areas of heart-stirring beauty without any of the long, and occasionally dreary slogs across nondescript moorland to be endured in parts of the northern Peak District, or again in Durham and Northumberland.

Exactly where the Yorkshire Dales begin as you

The Pennine Way above Horton — a walk along the backbone of England

follow the Way across the gritstone and acid moorland of the South Pennines and Brontë Country is open to speculation, but the charming valley of Lotherside, with its first hint of soft-grey limestone, and the subtle greens of more fertile pastures, has as good a claim as any.

A good starting point
For practical purposes the mill village of Cowling, with its twin hamlet of Ickornshaw, is a good starting point. On the main A6068 Colne-Keighley road, it has an hourly bus service between Keighley and Burnley. So it is quite simple to leave a car in Keighley to return on a choice of transport via Skipton.

From Ickornshaw, its name an evocative reminder of the oakwoods that once covered the Pennines (Ickorn = acorn) a mixture of lane and fieldpaths across soft pastures, across a little valley and a low hillock, bring you to Lothersdale.

The quiet valley that contains Lothersdale village will be the first real surprise and delight of this part of the Pennine Way. It is a mill village, and the mill has a mighty 45 foot waterwheel, now preserved as an important monument. The village post office welcomes walkers with tea, and there is a pleasant inn.

A climb to Pinhaw
The first real climb into the true Dales country now begins, at first a gentle ascent of a long green pasture, but soon a winding path across heather moorland to the craggy summit of Pinhaw Beacon. Pinhaw may be a mere 1273 feet high, but, if the weather is clear, the whole of the Yorkshire Dales unfolds before you – the magnificent limestone ridges above Malham, the peaks of Ingleborough and Pen-y-ghent and, over to the north-west the distant tops of the Langdale Pikes. Pinhaw was one of the chain of beacons which crossed northern England and was used in Tudor times to carry messages of major significance – such as the pending invasion by the Spanish Armada in 1588. Beamsley Beacon, across in Wharfedale is the next beacon in the chain.

Tracks and paths now descend to Thornton in Craven (hourly Ribble bus service to Skipton for Keighley) where the village shop supplies walkers with mugs of tea. Winding paths across farmland and low hillocks soon lead to the towpath of the 18th-century Leeds-Liverpool Canal and an extraordinary double arch bridge that still carries the thundering traffic of the A59. The Cross Keys Inn and the village shop supply refreshment.

Quiet, meandering paths which, in spite of waymarking, require careful map-reading (whoever described the Pennine Way as a 'pedestrian motorway' never walked the Way in this part of Craven) find their way across pasture, past little copses, across drumlins (low hills of glacial origin) into Gargrave.

A natural break

Gargrave makes a natural breaking point for the Pennine Way walker. The village is an old coaching town on the Leeds-Kendal road, now the A65, and has cafés, shops, pubs, an hourly bus service (Pennine Motors) into Skipton and a direct rail service from its little unstaffed station on the Leeds-Morecambe line to and from Keighley. After a 12 mile walk from Cowling, it's a natural end to a pleasant day to enjoy refreshment and await return transport from a greystone village whose little, unpretentious graveyard was the last resting place of a Chancellor of the Exchequer – the Rt. Hon. Ian Macleod.

The second stage

If Cowling to Gargrave makes a natural first stage of the Pennine Way in the Dales, the next stage might well be a leisurely seven mile stroll into Malham village. There are more of those lovely, low green hills to cross, the pale grey drystone walls and light, spongy pasture indicating the limestone bedrock of the soil. Nothing can compare with limestone country for the walker – dry underfoot, sweet scented in spring when wild flowers and herbs cover every bank, old barns and farmhouses that seem to have grown out of the very earth, and always as you walk north, the romantic turrets and crags of limestone on the far ridges.

You are soon following the infant River Aire, the river which, dark and sluggish, finds its way eventually through Leeds. Here it is bright, sparkling, following a shallow valley below Airton and Kirkby Malham, past an old mill or two where in less profligate times the energy of the river turned wheels of manufacture. It is the sign of these same times that the mills are now country cottages or flats for commuters or weekend visitors.

Historic Malham

Malham is an unpretentious little village in a magnificent setting, a great bowl of the hills which focuses on two great natural features – the massive Cove and the awe-inspiring Gordale Scar. If you arrive early in Malham, call in at the National Park Information Centre, close to where the Pennine Way enters the village, and learn something of the remarkable natural history of the area, where the effects of the faulting of the Great Scar Limestone has produced some of the finest examples of karst limestone scenery in the British Isles. Equally fascinating is the story of man's occupation of the area, from Bronze and Iron Age times (Iron Age fields can still be deciphered on the hillsides around the village, through monastic occupation to the modern hill farmer, coping with the pressure of the modern visitor invasion. If you have time before catching the late afternoon Pennine bus down the valley take the classic walk from the village past the Cove to Gordale (please do not climb the falls which already suffer severe problems of erosion) to Janet's Foss and back to the village.

Walkers pause on the limestone pavements above Malham Cove

On limestone pavements

The next stage from Malham might well be a long and strenuous one. It begins with an ascent of the side of the Cove, that magnificent natural ampitheatre of limestone which once carried a waterfall of Niagara-like proportions, to cross the limestone pavements of the summit (care required) – polished and eroded limestone whose clints (stones) and grikes (cracks) are a major feature of the Dales. The view from the pavement, down Malhamdale is quite ethereal, looking across to Pendle Hill in Lancashire.

A monastic track, Trougate, now takes the Pennine Way through craggy limestone pastures, evocatively named Prior Rakes (a sheep walk managed by the monks of Bolton Priory) to Malham Tarn, a beautiful, natural lake in a superb setting. Malham Tarn House at the edge of the lake, originally a shooting lodge of Lord Lister, was the country seat of Walter Morrison, Victorian philanthropist. The famous art critic and essayist John Ruskin was a frequent visitor here, as was Charles Kingsley, novelist, best remembered for *The Water Babies*, the didactic novel which owed much of its inspiration to Malham Tarn and the scenery of Malhamdale and nearby Littondale.

Field Studies Centre

The Pennine Way goes through the estate woodland, now a Nature Reserve, part of a scientific reserve of international importance. Tarn House is now a Field Studies Centre, a base for teaching and research of wide repute which offers a number of fascinating short and holiday courses, for the beginner as well as the expert, in various aspects of Dales natural and local history.

From the Tarn the Way swings northwards again, across more pasture, climbing close by Tennant Gill farm and the long, winding ascent of Fountains Fell. As its name implies, Fountains Fell was owned and managed, with its ring of outlying granges and farms, by the monks and lay brothers of Fountains Abbey, whose industry and expertise laid the foundations of the modern Yorkshire woollen industry, initially exporting wool via the Abbey to York and the Renaissance city states of Italy, later to develop the great West Riding manufacturing tradition.

Approaching Pen-y-ghent

If it is a dullish, steady climb up this great fellside, the summit cairns once reached afford superb views, most specially and dramatically across the Pennine Way's next major objective, Pen-y-ghent, which stands in majestic profile across the intervening valley. But tough, wild walking lies ahead, down the old miners' path to Dalehead, and the well used path up the shoulder of Pen-y-ghent, which soon becomes extremely steep.

By anyone's standards Pen-y-ghent is a real mountain. Though a mere 2273 feet, in form and ruggedness its mountain character is unmistakable, which anyone who struggles up the steep boulderfield to the flat summit plateau will appreciate. The view from the summit, in clear weather, is superb – across Ribblesdale, to Ingleborough and Whernside, the other two 'Three Peaks' to the head of Littondale, across to the Bowland hills of Lancashire. There is a sense of space and beauty about Pen-y-ghent, in good weather one of England's finest summits, its Celtic name signifying 'Hill of the Border' no doubt of the Celtic kingdom of Brigantia in pre-Roman times.

The ascent into Ribblesdale begins along a fine miner's track, but soon crosses one of the worst erosion problems of the Pennine Way, exacerbated by the Three Peaks Marathon walk, where the delicate peat surface has been damaged by the pressure of thousands of boots. Keep to the National Park boardwalks and causeways to help minimise the damage.

You soon pass Hunt Pot, an awesome natural fissure in the surface of the limestone, then descend Horton Scar Lane, a long stony track into Horton in Ribblesdale.

North from Horton

Though dominated by massive nearby quarries, Horton has many attractions for the walker, notably the excellent Pen-y-ghent Café in the village centre, which welcomes Pennine Way walkers, and the Crown Inn. Whaites' bus service will carry the weary walker back into Settle, with connecting bus service to Gargrave and Skipton for a parked car after what will have been a strenuous 15 mile day of fell and mountain walking.

From Horton northwards if you are using public transport you'll need to do a little research.

Signposts spur the weary walker on to Pen-y-ghent's distant summit

On certain weekends Dales Rail bus and train services link Horton Station with Hawes, whilst Ribble Motors have a summer weekend service between Settle, Horton and Hawes. The walking is easy enough, tracks and green ways on relatively easy gradients through fine countryside, 15 miles to Hawes.

This is a grand, wild landscape, its ruggedness relieved by beautiful gills where rowan and birch cling and in spring primroses flash their delicate beauty. You pass several small potholes, some with waterfalls and the occasional intrepid, wet-suited caver making his way down. From Ling Gill with its ancient bridge and Nature Reserve the Pennine Way climbs to the summit of Cam Fell along an ancient coach road where the Cam High Way, a Roman road, is followed to Kidhaw Gate. This is one of the great watersheds of England, with the source of the River Wharfe nearby on Cam Fell which eventually finds its way via the Humber into the North Sea and to the west, the source of the Ribble which emerges in the Irish Sea.

The Pennine Way strikes off the Roman Road along the side of Dodd Fell, grand views northwards now to Swarth Fell and the distinct and characteristic outline of Wild Boar Fell, reputedly where the last wild boar in England was shot, before descending to the village of Gayle and the little Wensleydale town of Hawes.

Hawes has great character, a busy market town (market day Tuesday) with shops, pubs, cafés, accommodation, the excellent Museum of Upper Dales Life and National Park Information Centre in the old station and weekend return bus to Skipton and Horton.

A spectacular waterfall

If Wensleydale is a dale to linger in, offering superb delights for the walker prepared to discover its secrets, the climb between the two valleys has much to offer.

It begins easily enough by fieldpath to Hardraw where a visit to Hardraw Force through the grounds of the Green Dragon Inn is not to be missed. This 96 foot high shimmering column of water is reputedly the highest above ground in England. Painted by Turner, it is in a natural rocky amphitheatre used every spring for a Brass

Top: Swaledale, one of the Way's finest views. Left: Lonely Tan Hill Inn north of Keld

Band Contest where bands throughout the north compete. The intrepid can actually stand behind the waterfall and enjoy the shimmering curtain of water, though expect some spray on your anorak.

From Hardraw begins the ascent of Great Shunner Fell, the gradient never steep. Initially the Way follows an old walled, stony lane, then crosses wild, boggy, peaty moor, churned up after rain. This is a remote and bleak summit, at 2340 feet higher than Pen-y-ghent but less dramatic, compensated, in good weather, by glorious views back to the Three Peaks, down both Wensleydale and, as you proceed northwards, into Swaledale.

Viking Villages

Swaledale is ample compensation for the ascent you have completed. You reach, by a long and stony track, the hamlet of Thwaite, its name as Viking as the early settlers of the valley. It was the birthplace of Richard and Cherry Kearton, pioneer wildlife photographers, and the Kearton Guesthouse has a justified national reputation for excellent food and accommodation – welcoming Pennine wayfarers.

Tom Stephenson, doyen of ramblers and originator of the Pennine Way, a man whose vision, imagination and dogged determination brought the Way into being, has confessed that there is no more beautiful part of the entire 270 mile route than that between Thwaite and Keld, as you ascend the side of Kisdon Hill to enjoy breathtakingly lovely views along Swaledale, across the village of Muker, clustered around its Elizabethan church. Little wonder that Swaledale has become enshrined, through the novels and films of the vet James Herriot as 'Herriot Country'; but its beauty is truly reserved for the walker, not the motorist or the coach tripper, as you will discover as you follow the Pennine Way up that hauntingly lovely hillside above the Swale past Kisdon and East Gill Force, to Keld, another Norse settlement and the last outpost of civilisation in this valley. You will have covered 13 miles from Hawes and on Saturdays between April and October there is a late afternoon bus to take you back to a parked car.

Lonely outstation

From Keld northwards there is no public transport to reach that lonely outstation of the Dales at Tan Hill, so as it is but six miles away, best to plan a circular return trip coming back by West Stonesdale, Robert's Seat and Raven's Seat. This is wild, empty countryside, some of the bleakest, loneliest and most fiercesome in England. Judge your arrival at Tan Hill Inn at opening time; apart from the moorland inn, with its own coal mine, there is no other human habitation.

Beyond Tan Hill there is a long wild tramp across even more rugged and desolate countryside until the delights of Teeside beyond Stainmoor Gap, stuff for the true Pennine Way devotee, but beyond the Yorkshire Dales.

If you are planning even a short walk on the Pennine Way in the Dales go well equipped – boots, rainwear, food, good maps, a compass. People have died of exposure on the tops. Leave word where you are going. Though waymarking is good, you must have large scale maps – at very least 1:50 000 *Landranger* series 103, 98, 92, preferably 1:25 000 *Outdoor Leisure Malham and Upper Wharfedale* and *The Three Peaks* for the sections from Gargrave to Hawes. Tom Stephenson's HMSO Guide is invaluable, as is Alfred Wainwright's classic *A Pennine Way Companion*.

USEFUL ADDRESSES:

Ramblers Association, *1/5 Wandsworth Road, London SW8 2LJ*
Pennine Way Council, *Hon. Sec, CDJ Sainty, 89 Radford Road, London SE13 6SB*

BUS SERVICES:

Service 25 (also Dales Rail) Keighley – Colne: *WYPTE, Metro House, West Parade, Wakefield, West Yorkshire*
Service 743 Colne – Thornton – Skipton; Burnley – Settle – Hawes: *Ribble Motor Services, Frenchwood Avenue, Preston, Lancs.*
Skipton – Gargrave – Malham; Settle – Gargrave – Skipton: *Pennine Motors, Gargrave, Skipton, North Yorkshire*
Horton – Settle: *DW Waites, 6 Halsteads Terrace, Settle, North Yorkshire*
Service 800 Keld – Hawes: *West Yorkshire Road Co, PO Box 24, East Parade, Harrogate*

YORKSHIRE DALES

Gazetteer

Each entry in this Gazetteer has the atlas page number on which the place can be found and/or its National Grid reference included under the heading. An explanation of how to use the National Grid is given on page 74.

Above: The River Aire on its gentle course through Airton

Arkengarthdale's hexagonal Powder House was built in 1807 to store gunpowder used in the mines

Appletreewick

Map Ref: 96SE0560

On the east side of Wharfedale two miles below Burnsall, and locally called 'Aptrick', the village prospered from 1300 when Bolton Priory acquired its manor with its extensive sheep ranges and valuable lead mines. Charters for markets and a fair were granted, and the fair remained important until the impact of the railways in the mid-19th century.

Stone houses line the steep, attractive main street between High Hall at the top and Low Hall at the bottom. The Tudor-style High Hall was restored by Sir William Craven, Appletreewick's own 'Dick Whittington', who became Sheriff and Lord Mayor of London at the beginning of the 17th century. He was born in a cottage almost opposite, one of a pair converted into St John's church, 1897–98, as a chapel-of-ease to Burnsall. Lower down is Monks' Hall, largely rebuilt in 1697 on the site of Bolton Priory's grange.

Arncliffe's porched barn and houses seen across the village green

This house has a projecting wing with an unusual façade, its door reached by an outside stair, and upper windows whose lintels are adorned with semi-circles, and pigeon-holes over the doorway and windows.

Arkengarthdale

Map Ref: NY9507 to SE0499

Arkengarthdale is Yorkshire's most northerly Pennine dale. Its place-names – Arkle Town, Langthwaite, Eskeleth, Whaw and Booze – speak of Norse settlement but its landscape is scarred with the remains of 18th- and 19th-century lead-mining, touching the green valley with melancholy. Born on the lonely fells, the Arkle Beck's short but lively course takes it south-eastwards from near Tan Hill to its meeting with the Swale at Grinton.

Travelling up the dale from Reeth, the inviting moorland road passes Arkle Town, the first hamlet, formerly with parish church, inn and workhouse. Now there are none of these. Langthwaite's huddle of grey stone houses form the focal-point of the dale, with pub, shop, and unusual 'Waterloo' church of 1817, one of many then built with money provided by Parliament in an attempt to counteract atheism and free-thinking threatening the Established Church after the French Revolution.

Beyond Langthwaite is CB, the only place-name in England composed of initials. They commemorate Charles Bathurst, grandson of Dr John Bathurst, Oliver Cromwell's physician, who bought the Manor of Arkengarthdale in 1656 and developed the lead-mines. The family connection continued until 1912. In a field by the road which turns off northwards to climb the Stang, heading for Barnard Castle, is the elegant, hexagonal Powder House of 1807, built to store gunpowder used in the mines. Near the CB Hotel a narrow road turns off to climb steeply past old spoil-heaps to cross the moors into Swaledale, negotiating on the way a water-splash in one moorland valley, and Surrender Bridge and the Hard Level Gill in another, in both of which broad areas of fine green turf offer suitable parking-places close to chuckling becks.

Back in Arkengarthdale the road continues to the head of the dale, passing the last hamlet, Whaw, and climbing steadily to the lonely Pennine heights by Tan Hill Inn, England's highest pub, 1732 feet, where one road branches off to Keld in Swaledale, and another heads westwards over the fells to Brough and Kirkby Stephen.

Arncliffe

Map Ref: 91SD9371

Of Littondale's four settlements Arncliffe is the largest, and the only one on the south side of the valley, approached most easily from the

B6160 up Wharfedale by a minor road a mile beyond Kilnsey. Splendidly situated on a well-drained gravel delta above the flood-plain of the River Skirfare, Arncliffe's houses, cottages, farms and barns face inwards to a spacious green, outwards to green hillsides etched with long limestone scars. One barn on the north side of the green is a good example of the local style, with a porched entrance, and a datestone of 1677. Behind the village buildings are small crofts, almost one to each house, beyond them limestone walls climb the surrounding hills separating higher fields, and the common pastures extend to the darker gritstone moors.

St Oswald's church lies close to the river north of the village, and the road up the dale crosses the river past Bridge End where Charles Kingsley was a visitor, to Old Cotes, a graceful house of 1650 whose gabled porch has a 3-light window characteristic of late 17th-century houses in this area of the dales. A narrow, winding road climbs steeply southwards from Arncliffe across the fells to Malham, an invitation to the heart of Craven.

AA recommends:
Hotels: Amerdale House, I-star, Country House Hotel, tel. Arncliffe 250

Askrigg

Map Ref: 85SD9491

Most dales' villages sit comfortably at the foot of sheltering fells and Askrigg is no exception. Seen across Wensleydale from the main A684 five miles east of Hawes it is dominated by Ellerkin and Askrigg Common rising behind it. The minor road along the valley's northern side winds through the village, whose main street is bordered by stone houses in almost continuous rows, elegant three-storey ones presenting an almost urban appearance. Most are of 18th- and 19th-century date, arising from Askrigg's increasing prosperity through its clock-making, lead-mining and textiles, and the Richmond-Lancaster Turnpike which came through the village in 1751.

The street widens near the 15th-century parish church, and has a market-cross at its focal-point and an iron bull-ring in the cobbles. Opposite is Cringley House, the 'Skeldale House' of the vet James Herriot in the BBC TV series *All Creatures Great and Small.* This is now an Abbeyfield Home – one of many ambitious community projects of the Askrigg Foundation, a charitable trust set up in 1971 with the initiative of Malcolm Stonestreet, then Vicar of Askrigg. Low Mill, an Outdoor Pursuits Centre for youngsters, with a recent extension for disabled people, and the Craft Shop, are other successful projects of the Foundation.

The living and the dead face each other in Askrigg's main street

North of the church is a row of 17th-century houses, with a lane leading to an attractive short walk to the woods and waterfalls of Mill Gill and Whitfield Gill. Two miles east of Askrigg is Nappa Hall, a 15th-century fortified house (not open) whose towers can be seen from the road, while a public path passes close to it. West of the village the road continues up Wensleydale to Bainbridge and Hawes, while to the north exciting moorland roads cross the watershed to Swaledale.

AA recommends:
Hotels: King's Arms, Market Place, 2-star, tel. Wensleydale 50258

A set from the TV series All Creatures Great and Small *in Richmond Museum*

James Herriot Country

The world's most famous vet had his surgery in Darrowby, non-existent on any map of Yorkshire. It is a composite place, part imaginary but with strong flavours of Thirsk – where his practice still operates – Richmond, Leyburn and Middleham. To their west is the 'Herriot Country' of the Dales including all of Swaledale and Wensleydale with its tributary valleys of Raydale, Bishopdale, Walden and Coverdale. Herriot's practice did not take him over the watershed into Wharfedale or into the western dales beyond Hawes; his country was the land of soaring fells, bare hillsides, stone walls, barns, farms and friendly villages of the northern dales, the area selected by the BBC for location filming of their successful television series of Herriot's books, *All Creatures Great and Small.*

Askrigg became 'Darrowby', with Cringley House in the centre of the village, now an Abbeyfield Home, the 'Skeldale House' surgery-home of Siegfried Farnon, Tristan, and James and Helen Herriot. Dales farms, especially the more remote ones, provided the authentic setting for many delightful sequences, illustrating for millions of viewers throughout the world the unique, often austere, sometimes intimate, beauty of the Yorkshire Dales. For thousands of visitors now, 'Herriot Country' is as important as Brontë Country.

It is very real. The places and the people are real. You meet them in the villages, at the markets, on the farms. You can enjoy a drink at the Wheatsheaf Inn at Carperby where James and Helen spent their working honeymoon in a pre-war November; or in the Wensleydale Heifer at West Witton where they enjoyed so many meals; you can appreciate the quiet charms of Coverdale, where they spent happy holidays at West Scrafton; you can even drive through the same watersplash on the moor road between Swaledale and Arkengarthdale featured in the title sequence of the BBC series which introduced Herriot's Yorkshire to an enthralled audience.

Austwick

Map Ref: 89SD7668

About five miles north-west of Settle
and just off the busy A65, grey stone
houses face small greens or border
narrow lanes. The green hills and
limestone country north of the village
are its chief attractions. The head of
this quiet, remote valley is a gem of
limestone scenery, with clean white
scars, outcrops and pavements.
Nearer to Austwick, and reached by
easy tracks from Thwaite Lane or the
Crummackdale lane, is Norber, a
limestone hill on whose lower slopes
are littered large numbers of dark,
massive rocks. These are the famous
Norber Boulders – in geological
terms 'glacial erratics' – carried by a
glacier during the late Ice Age from a
source half a mile up the valley and
dumped on this limestone plateau.
Being harder than the rock beneath
they have resisted erosion by rain and
wind, while the rock beneath has
been worn away leaving the huge
boulders perched on small pedestals
of white limestone.

AA recommends:
Hotels: Traddock, I-star, *tel.* Clapham
224
Guesthouses: Rawlinshaw (farmhouse),
tel. Settle 3214

*A Norber Boulder, perched on its white
limestone pedestal near Austwick. Views
from here are superb*

Aysgarth

Map Ref: 86SE0188

Aysgarth is in two parts. The village
itself is on the main road to
Wensleydale, the A684, and has no
particular distinction. Over half a
mile to the east, near Palmer Flatts,
the Youth Hostel and the church, a
short, steep hill descends to the river,
crosses by a narrow stone bridge,
climbs the northern bank to the
National Park Information Centre
and car park, and eventually links up
with the minor road along the north
side of the valley. The main
attraction is undoubtedly Aysgarth

Force, where the River Ure, confined
between wooded banks, falls over a
series of broad, shallow terraces in a
system extending over a mile. The
Upper Falls, easily seen from the
bridge and roadside, have the most
beautiful setting; to view the Middle
and Lower Falls – the most dramatic
– it is necessary to follow public
footpaths, well-signposted, through
Freeholders' Wood. Recent
improvements to these, and the
construction of a viewing platform by
Lower Falls, make it possible for
disabled visitors in wheelchairs to
appreciate the scene. The track
through Freeholders' Wood is very
muddy in wet weather when, of
course, the falls are at their best.

Freeholders' Wood is now owned
by the National Park Authority, but
its freeholders, mainly people in
Carperby, retain certain common
rights, including that of gathering
wood. In co-operation with them the
National Park has started a 15-year
programme of coppicing the hazel.
This involves cutting trees just above
ground level, when the 'stools' then
throw up new shoots which will
subsequently be large enough to cut
in 7–15 years. Managed coppicing is
rare in the north of England. Two
separate areas of under one acre each
are to be coppiced each year, and a
start has been made.

Below Aysgarth bridge, which was
widened by John Carr in 1788, is
Yore Mill. Built 1784–85 as a corn
mill it had become ruinous by 1822,
quickly repaired and used as a corn
and worsted mill, but was up for sale
by 1851 and destroyed by fire two
years later. Rebuilt immediately to

*Majestic against a bank of trees the
Upper Falls (left) tumble downstream
into the Middle Falls (below) at Aysgarth*

twice the original size it subsequently had a variety of uses, being a flour-mill from 1912–59. Since 1967 its roomy interior has housed the Coach and Carriage Museum. Above the mill St Andrew's church is largely a rebuilding of 1866, its 4½-acre churchyard indicating its earlier importance as the mother-church for the whole of upper Wensleydale. The former 81,000 acre parish of Aysgarth is now sub-divided. Inside the church, the exquisite wooden screen filling the south side of the chancel was brought to Aysgarth from Jervaulx Abbey at the Dissolution of the Monasteries. It was carved about 1506 by members of the famous Ripon school of carvers. At its western end is the delicately-carved Vicar's stall made from two bench-ends from Jervaulx.

AA recommends:
Hotels: Palmer Flatt, I-star, *tel.* Aysgarth 228
Garages: HBS Motors, *tel.* Aysgarth 209

Bainbridge

Map Ref: 85SD9390

The Romans came to Bainbridge about AD80 and established a succession of forts on Brough Hill, a natural grassy hillock to the east of the village, occupying the site almost continuously for over 300 years. It gives a fine view of Wensleydale and of Bainbridge village whose grey stone houses are set round the edge of a large rectangular green, gay with daffodils in spring, sheep-grazed in the summer. Stocks are a reminder of past punishment, and the custom of horn-blowing between Holy Rood (27 September) and Shrovetide in early spring dates from the Middle Ages when Bainbridge was on the edge of a hunting forest of Wensleydale. Unfortunately the custom is now only occasionally carried out.

Villagers bought the manorial rights of Bainbridge from the City of London in the late 17th century and its affairs are in the hands of its locally-elected Lords Trustees who ensure, among other things, that the green is well-maintained. Although the Rose and Crown overlooking the green is dated 1443 its present appearance suggests an early 19th-century building. Unusually, Bainbridge has no Anglican church, but does have a Chapel and a Friends' Meeting House. Low Mill, on the east side of the green, has recently been restored, together with its fine water-wheel, and is occasionally open to visitors. England's shortest named river, the Bain, drains from Semer Water into a steep, two-mile course, entering Bainbridge over a fine cascade of waterfalls above the main road, and flowing down the eastern edge of the village into the River Ure.

AA recommends:
Hotels: Rose and Crown, Village Green, 2-star, *tel.* Wensleydale 50225

Waterfalls

A 19th-century engraving of Hardraw Force

Water there is in plenty in the Dales, and where rivers and becks flow over different rock strata, eroding them at different rates, waterfalls are formed. Each main valley has its falls, with Wensleydale having the greatest number and most variety, although upper Swaledale has a concentration of falls around Keld.

Aysgarth Force, in mid-Wensleydale, is the most famous, for size and scenic beauty, with the River Ure tumbling over a series of terraces spaced out for a mile between wooded banks. Further down the river Redmire Force is far less spectacular and little-visited, but by West Burton village in lower Bishopdale Burton Falls make a charming scene above a narrow packhorse bridge. Above Askrigg, and reached by a footpath from near the church, Mill Gill and Whitfield Gill falls are the highest waterfalls in one of the finest gill woods in the Dales, with leaps of 60 feet, bettered only by Hardraw Force, near Hawes, access to which is through a pub, the Green Dragon, at Hardraw. Set in a natural amphitheatre, Hardraw Force throws a shimmering curtain of water into a deep pool, and the adventurous can walk behind the fall. Two miles beyond Hawes Cotter Force is easily approached by public footpath, and is a charming little fall.

Above Keld the River Swale falls over broad ledges at Wain Wath Force but narrows into a more forceful leap at Kisdon Force some distance below the village. Nearer the village, and by the Pennine Way, East Gill Falls take a lively beck over a series of cataracts into the Swale. Waterfalls in Wharfedale take the river over limestone ledges in an attractive roadside setting two miles above Hubberholme, while near Grassington a much heavier flow gives some sound and fury to Linton Falls crossed by an iron footbridge. Near Malham, Janet's Foss is reached by an easy and pleasant walk, while Ingleton can claim in its famous 'glens' (charge made) a fine series of waterfalls linked by a popular footpath culminating at Thornton Force.

Bishopdale

Map Ref: SD9580 to SE0289

Three roads cross the watershed between Wensleydale and Wharfedale, from Hawes, Aysgarth and Middleham. The B6160 from near Aysgarth is the easiest road, threading its way up Bishopdale, the largest of Wensleydale's tributary valleys, a mile wide at its lower end and narrowing towards its head at Kidstones Pass, six miles away. Of the three villages broadly spaced at the foot of Bishopdale, West Burton dispersed around its large rectangular green is the most beautiful and the best-known; Thoralby is more compact, with a smaller green and some fine 17th-century farmhouses, while Newbiggin remains aloof, just off the B6160 near Street Head Inn, and is a small, linear village which ends at a farmyard.

In Ice Age times Bishopdale was filled with a glacial lake and the deposited silt has given the valley a fertile soil. During the Middle Ages, when Bishopdale formed part of the Honour of Middleham, it was preserved as a hunting chase for deer, but after Middleham's ownership ended early in the 17th century it became possible for tenant farmers eventually to acquire their own holdings, and as yeomen they began to rebuild their homes. As a result Bishopdale probably has some of the finest 17th-century farmhouses in the Yorkshire Dales, many of them distinguished with decorated dated doorheads. Good examples of these buildings are to be seen at Thoralby and Newbiggin,

West New House at Bishopdale, built in 1635

while nearer the head of the valley West New House (1635), and Smelter (1701), though off the road, have public footpaths passing close to them. Bishopdale's unusual orientation, NE-SW, has resulted in many of the farms on the east side of the valley being built to face south-east to catch the morning sun, and hence showing only their backs to the road. Smelter is one of these, but West New House opposite shows its fine 'long-house' frontage to perfection.

At West Burton Bishopdale divides, the main valley continuing south-west and the smaller valley of Walden entering from the south. Lanes leave West Burton to traverse each side of Walden but not joining at the valley head. There is no road out of the valley, which is dominated by the mountain of Buckden Pike.

Bolton Abbey

Map Ref: 97SE0753

Through long usage this Wharfedale village on the B6160 has become called Bolton Abbey although its famous ruins are those of a priory. Founded at Embsay in 1120 it moved to its present site in 1154, largely completed by 1220, with later additions. The west tower was started in 1520 but not finished, as a result of the Dissolution. However, after three years' recent work, the tower has windows glazed for the first time in 450 years and now has a roof with laminated timbers. The floor of the tower is to become a reception area for visitors. The nave of the priory church was allowed to remain in use as the parish church, whose 13th-century west front is a fine

Religious Sites

For almost four centuries various monasteries extended their influence over the Yorkshire Dales and transformed huge areas of it. Cistercian monks, bringing with them great sheep-breeding skills, founded Fountains Abbey near Ripon in 1132, Jervaulx Abbey in Wensleydale in 1145. Augustinian canons settled at Bolton Priory in Wharfedale in 1155, while smaller foundations were established at Coverham in Wensleydale in 1202, and at Easby near Richmond in 1152.

Of these Fountains Abbey (National Trust) is by far the most important, probably the outstanding Cistercian monastic ruin in existence, both for its church and its claustral buildings. At Jervaulx (privately owned; public admitted) the dormitory and chapter-house ruins are impressive, while Bolton Priory is not only hauntingly beautiful in its setting, but displays superb Early English architecture. Coverham shows two bays of its nave arcade, and fragments of masonry incorporated into later buildings, while Easby's pride is its refectory (Department of Environment).

An engraver's impression of the interior of Fountains Abbey

Richmond's glory is the splendid 15th-century bell-tower of the former Franciscan friary, north of the Market Place, while above the river to the south there are fragments of a tiny priory. The road to Reeth, through lower Swaledale, passes the ruined tower of a very poor 13th-century Cistercian nunnery of Ellerton Priory, while beyond, on the opposite side of the river, very little survives of the church of a small Benedictine nunnery of Marrick Priory, and part of the building has been converted into use as a Diocesan Outdoor Pursuits Centre.

Brimham Rocks – blocks of dark Millstone Grit worn into strange shapes

example of early English architecture. The setting of the priory ruin is superb – riverside meadows, woodlands, moors and hills – so it is not surprising that it has inspired famous artists including Turner, Girtin and Landseer. Romillys, Cliffords and Percys have been dominating influences in Wharfedale from Norman times to the 17th century, when a Clifford heiress married the first Earl of Burlington. The last descendant of this family married in 1748 a Duke of Devonshire, whose family has owned the Bolton Abbey estates until the present time, and developments by Burlington and the Devonshires have resulted in the beautiful parkland quality of this part of Wharfedale.

Bolton Hall to the west of the priory incorporates the 14th-century priory gatehouse into 19th-century extensions. Nearby, an archway over the road was an 18th-century aqueduct which carried water to a mill, and just off the road is a splendid tithe barn. Miles of public paths are an encouragement to explore Bolton Woods and the parkland, and a short way up the valley is the Strid, a narrow gorge where the Wharfe surges swiftly, 30 feet deep, between rocky banks. A self-guiding Nature Trail explains various aspects of the wildlife. Car parking for Bolton Abbey, its parkland, and Strid Woods is available only at fee-paying car parks. There is no roadside parking.

The beautifully-situated ruin of Barden Tower, three miles up Wharfedale from Bolton Abbey, was built in 1485 by Lord Henry Clifford, and restored by Lady Anne Clifford in 1658–59, falling into disrepair in the early 19th century, but is still an impressive, three-storey tower-house. Chapel House across the yard, probably built in the 15th-century as a chapel and priest's house, was later adapted to farmhouse use. Recent restoration has turned it into a small guesthouse and restaurant, while nearby a splendid barn has been converted into a Bunkhouse Barn providing simple, self-catering overnight accommodation.

AA recommends:
Hotels: Devonshire Arms, 3-star, *tel.* Bolton Abbey 441

Brimham Rocks

Map Ref: 77SE2164

Outside the National Park area but still very much part of the Yorkshire Dales, Brimham Rocks lie between the B6265 Ripon-Pateley Bridge road and the B6165 Harrogate-Pateley Bridge road. Almost 400 acres of moorland contain, in an area of about 50 acres, a unique piece of British scenery. Fretted, eroded

pillars and blocks of dark Millstone Grit protrude from the bedrock to heights of 20 feet or more. Worn by weather into fantastic shapes they have fascinated since the 18th century. Victorian tourists gave fanciful names to many – Sphinx, Turtle, Dancing Bear, Idol, Anvil, Castle, Pulpit, Druid's Altar – and the grotesque shapes are enhanced by their setting among silver birches, bracken and heather. The National Trust now owns Brimham (car park charge) and has improved many footpaths among the rocks. A shop and Information Centre have been provided in Brimham House, a quarter of a mile from the car park. No vehicles are allowed in the area of the rocks themselves, so visitors need to be prepared to walk. Wheelchair access is straightforward, and all-weather paths have recently been completed.

Burnsall

Map Ref: 96SE0361

Wharfedale's landscape changes at Burnsall. Above the village are the distinctive limestone uplands, with gleaming scars and hillsides patterned with white walls; below Burnsall the valley becomes more wooded, gritstone walls are dark lines in the landscape, and the moorland skylines more sombre. The B6160 coming up Wharfedale from Bolton Bridge enters Burnsall near a riverside car park (charge) and winds its way between mellow stone houses of 17th- and 18th-century date, many with mullioned windows. Near the top of the street is St Wilfrid's church, approached through a 17th-century tapsel gate – a lychgate with a revolving 'turnstile' entrance. The church was largely rebuilt during the reign of Henry VIII but shows some 14th-century work including a beautiful, sculptured alabaster panel showing the Adoration of the Magi.

Evidence of a much older foundation is demonstrated by the crudely carved Norman font, fragments of Anglo-Danish crosses of the 9th or 10th centuries, and two hogback tombstones of the same date.

Adoration of the Magi, Burnsall Church

In the south aisle a tablet commemorates Sir William Craven who, in 1612 at his own expense, 'repaired and butified' the church, rebuilt Burnsall bridge, and the grammar school just below the church, which he had founded in 1602. It continued as a grammar-school until 1876 and is now used as a primary school. Its appearance is that of a small manor-house, with a two-storeyed gabled porch and mullioned windows with leaded lights.

Exploring the riverside paths to Appletreewick, Hebden and Grassington and field paths to Thorpe are the best ways to see the beautiful Wharfedale countryside.

AA recommends:
Hotels: Fell, 2-star, *tel.* Burnsall 209
Red Lion, 2-star, *tel.* Burnsall 204
Guesthouses: Manor House, *tel.* Burnsall 231

Dales Barns

Apart from the farmhouse, often with its barn or shippon adjoining and under the same roof, the traditional Dales building is a detached stone barn in the fields. This provided winter accommodation (mid-November to early May) for a small number of cows or younger stock. Hay for their feed was stored in the loft above, rationed out daily, and the cows milked daily at the barn. Manure was returned to the nearby meadows which yielded the hay.

Changes have occurred. Many hay-meadows have in the past reverted to permanent pasture. Current practices – often arising from and involving farm amalgamation, a change from hay to silage, the winter concentration of cattle in big new structures near the farmhouse – have caused many field barns to become redundant. Those situated close to villages and roads, and accompanying mains services, can sometimes be given a new lease of life through conversion into dwellings, but where this happens they lose their identity.

Between 1978 and 1982 the Yorkshire Dales National Park Committee, together with the Countryside Commission, converted five barns to provide overnight, self-catering

A stone barn near Hawes in Wensleydale

accommodation for visitors walking in the Dales. Each barn is conveniently situated in an interesting locality or close to a popular walking route such as the Pennine Way or the Dales Way. Each barn provides space heating and hot water, showers, wash-basins, toilets, a drying-room, as well as cooking and eating facilities, and bunk-beds in separate bedroom units. Barns can accept individuals, families or groups, who use the buildings as a base for local exploration or as part of a network. Car parking is available.

Bookings for barns can be made through the barn operator – usually the farmer, from whom dairy produce and other provisions can be ordered in advance. Costs are about £3 per adult per night, and details, with booking forms, are available from National Park Centres and Offices at Grassington and Bainbridge. The barns are at Barden Tower, Cam Houses (near the Pennine and Dales Ways), Catholes (Sedbergh), Dub-Cote (Horton in Ribblesdale), and Grange Farm, Buckden.

Carperby

Map Ref: 86SE0089

The minor road along the north side of Wensleydale passes through Carperby, where houses straggle along each side of the single street which widens towards the western end into a green. In the centre a high-stepped cross, dated 1674, tells of the time when Carperby had a market (granted in 1305). In the 17th century the village became an important Wensleydale centre of Quakerism, and its biggest building today is the Classically-styled Friends' Meeting House of 1864. The name of the Wheatsheaf Hotel suggests a corn-growing agriculture in the past, while the inn itself was

where James Herriot and his bride spent their honeymoon in the 1930s.

Between Carperby and Castle Bolton are excellent examples of lynchets – Saxon or medieval cultivation terraces in 'flights' of five or six, each terrace representing the deliberate levelling-out of part of a hillside to provide flat strips of land suitable for ploughing and the growing of corn. From near the middle of the village a lane leads northwards to the village stone quarry and the peat moors beyond, while to the south field paths lead to Freeholders' Wood by Aysgarth Falls, and to Redmire.

Castle Bolton

Map Ref: 86SE0391

This is the name of the village, hill-perched on the north side of Wensleydale six miles west of Leyburn, half a mile north of the minor road up the valley. Unpretentious stone cottages line its single street along a green, with a water-trough at one end and the massive ruins of Bolton Castle at the other. Wensleydale's largest and most splendidly-sited building was erected by the first Lord Scrope, Chancellor of England, in 1379, more as a fortified manor-house, with the needs of comfort predominating over those of defence. Designed with a huge, five-storey tower at each corner, four ranges of

The Friends' Meeting House at Carperby, once an important centre for Quakerism

living quarters enclosing a courtyard, and turrets in the middle of each of the two longer sides, it took 18 years to complete. The original gatehouse entrance was in the east curtain wall but visitors now enter via an outside stairway on the west. The antiquary, Leland, writing in about 1546, asserted that it cost £12,000 to build, an enormous sum equivalent to about £1½ million today.

From July 1568 until January 1569 the unhappy Mary, Queen of Scots, was imprisoned at Bolton – in some degree of comfort, it must be said, with about twenty servants billeted in the village. She herself is thought to have occupied a large room in the south-west tower, with a fireplace, and steps leading to her bedroom. Bolton Castle was garrisoned for the Royalists during the Civil War, besieged by the Parliamentary forces in 1645 and eventually surrendered. Two years later it was partially dismantled, and in 1761 the north-east tower, weakened a century earlier, fell during a great storm. The other three towers and the curtain walls survive almost to their original height. Owned by Lord Bolton the castle is open to the public, houses a folk museum of local history exhibits, and a good-quality restaurant. Opposite, and completely dwarfed by the castle, is St Oswald's church, part of which during each summer displays an interpretative exhibition of some aspect of Wensleydale's history or wildlife. There is a convenient car park (honesty-box) adjoining, and from the eastern end of the village a moor road climbs over to Grinton in Swaledale.

Clapham

Map Ref: 89SD7469

Now by-passed by the A65 between Settle and Ingleton as it skirts the southern flanks of Ingleborough, Clapham has three claims to fame, one scientific, one botanical and one literary. James Faraday was the village blacksmith and the father of Michael Faraday, pioneer of electrical science; Reginald Farrer travelled the world in search of plants, and from the Far East introduced many new species into Britain and Europe; and in April 1939 a monthly magazine, the *Yorkshire Dalesman*, was founded in Clapham. Now simply *The Dalesman* it is the most widely read and successful regional magazine in Britain. Its editorial office, and headquarters of the Dalesman Publishing Company with over 300 titles to its credit, is a stone building behind the houses on the west side of the village.

More wooded than most Dales villages Clapham is blessed with a beck flowing down the centre, dividing the two roads and houses which border them, and in its progress through Clapham crossed by four bridges. At the top of the village St James' church is, apart from its Perpendicular tower, a 19th-century rebuilding. Clapham is largely an estate-village of the Farrers who, coming to the area in the early 18th century, added to their estates, rebuilt Ingleborough Hall early last century, planted Clapham Gill with thousands of trees – larch, pine, spruce and hardwoods – dammed the beck to create a lake, and transformed the top part of the village near the church in the 1830s. Roads were re-routed, and short tunnels constructed which still lead under estate grounds as rights-of-way to Austwick and Selside. The Farrers explored and opened up Ingleborough Cave in 1837, and the family's dedication to natural history, culminating with Reginald Farrer's exploits during his short life (1881–1920) are commemorated in the Reginald Farrer Nature Trail, established in 1970. The National Park Centre and car park on the east side of the village are used by thousands of visitors each year, for many of whom Clapham is an excellent base from which to explore, on foot, the many varied aspects of the limestone landscape immediately north of the village.

AA recommends:
Restaurants: Goat Gap, I-fork, *tel.* Ingleton 41230
Garages: Clapham (E S Hartley), *tel.* Clapham 247 (day) and Bentham 62208 (night)

Coverham Bridge sweeps over the River Cover in Coverdale, a dale where riding stables are as big as hamlets and horses are exercised on local lanes

Conistone

Map Ref: 96SD9867

A narrow, winding road along the eastern side of Wharfedale between Grassington and Kettlewell is joined at Conistone by a link across the river from Kilnsey. Loosely grouped round a small green and along the road to Grassington, farmhouses, barns and houses are built of local limestone, with rendered walls and dressings of sandstone. Its Anglian (8th-century) pattern of settlement and farming is easily recognised, with meadowland by the river, arable fields with strip lynchets along the lower slopes of the hills, and common pastures above the limestone scars. Different stages of enclosure walls can also be identified, older ones uneven and curving, those of the late 18th century straight on the ground because they were planned on paper. Conistone's farmhouses and barns are mainly of the late 17th century, some of the latter having been recently converted, with great care and taste, into private houses.

Coverdale

Map Ref: SD9876 to SE1386

Within the National Park area Coverdale is the most easterly of Wensleydale's feeder valleys in the south. From East Witton and Middleham on the A6108, and from Wensley and West Witton on the A684, narrow lanes converge on lower Coverdale from Coverham to Melmerby, then head south-westwards into the wilder upper reaches of the valley before climbing to 1650 feet and crossing into Wharfedale at Kettlewell, with a very steep descent at Park Rash.

Formerly part of the Honour of Middleham Coverdale has the fragments of an abbey, a parish church, two chapels-of-ease, seven townships and many hamlets and farms. The few remains of Coverham Abbey are in private grounds, but a right-of-way along a lane through the

A Conistone farmyard

old gatehouse does allow a close view, especially of the former Guest House, now incorporated into a later house. Coverham Bridge throws a high single arch over the wooded River Cover, and Coverham church nearby is over-restored.

On the south side of the valley from the bridge a narrow road leads past Caldbergh to West Scrafton, to join the main road beyond Carlton. This comes up the north side with a branch to Melmerby. Carlton is Coverdale's principal village, with some good 17th-century houses. One building has a prominent inscription on the wall above the door indicating it was the home of Henry Constantine, a 19th-century local dialect poet. Beyond Carlton the valley is known as the High Dale, with Horsehouse three miles farther on, its community focus. The name is said to originate from the fact that it was a resting-place for packhorses on their journey from Wharfedale to Middleham. From here it is almost six miles to the top of the watershed, the road passing through the hamlets of Braidley and Woodale into wilder scenery, and it is hard to realise that, according to Ogilby's map of 1675, this route formed part of the important road from London to Richmond, via Skipton, Kettlewell and Middleham.

The Sun Inn at Dent is popular with visitors. It is a local meeting place

Dent and Dentdale

Map Ref: SD7784 to SD6491

It is as though a Cornish fishing-village has taken root amid the soaring fells of the Yorkshire Dales – although the village is now in Cumbria. There is no easy way to Dent. From the east the sensible approach is from the B6255 Hawes-Ingleton road near Newby Head. Soon a twisting descent takes you beneath the towering arches of Dent Head viaduct into the charming valley of the River Dee. At Lea Yeat this swings westwards into the pastoral landscape of Dentdale, with the better road along the north side of the valley, reaching Dent in four miles. An alternative eastern approach, not suitable for nervous motorists, leaves the A684 Hawes-Sedbergh road at Garsdale Head, climbs to 1760 feet before the long descent to Dent station (the highest main-line station in Britain at 1150 feet), and joins the valley road at Lea Yeat. From the west Sedbergh is the only gateway to lower Dentdale, while from Ingleton and Kirkby Lonsdale narrow moorland roads offer navigational challenges and scenic rewards.

Jervaulx Abbey ruins lie calm and tranquil in a wooded park at East Witton

A spacious car park on the west of the village (honesty-box) enjoys a magnificent view and makes it easy to explore this fascinating village on foot. Narrow winding streets are cobble-carpeted from wall to wall. Sturdy stone cottages sit snugly beneath low-pitched roofs of heavy, dark stone slabs. Colour-wash, mainly white, relieves the dark tones of stone quarried locally, and hides its poorer quality compared with that of the main dales. Chimneys, often perched on corbelled stacks, rise above rooftops, creating a close-viewed serrated skyline against distant green hills. Black paint outlines the shapes of windows, adding pattern to the intimacy of friendly streets.

The Sun Inn smiles across a corner to St Andrew's church whose long, low profile and dated clock look down protectively on a neat church-yard with good views up the dale. Inside, Jacobean box-pews in the south aisle and shiny brass memorials to the Sedgwick family are focal-points of interest. Near the southern entrance to the churchyard where three streets meet, is the main focus of the village, a rough-hewn block of pink Shap granite, perpetually spouting water, a memorial to Dent's most famous son, Adam Sedgwick, one of the greatest English geologists, whose father was the Vicar in the 18th century, and who attended Dent Grammar School, a tiny building adjoining the north side of the churchyard.

First-floor spinning-galleries were once a feature of houses in Dent and farms in the valley, used by women and girls of the households to spin yarn from the shorn fleeces of sheep. Dent itself gained a reputation in the 17th and 18th centuries for its thriving cottage industry of knitting, usually of simple garments like stockings, gloves, waistcoats and caps, carried out by all members of a family in order to supplement meagre incomes. Dent women continued to knit, commercially, until late last century, and Kendal remained the main market for the products, as it always had been. The Dales Way, a long-distance footpath between Ilkley and Windermere, passes through the whole length of Dentdale, often as an attractive riverside path.

AA recommends:
Self Catering: Seedsgill Barn (flat), *tel.* Dent 362
Garages: L Haygarth, *tel.* Dent 202 (day) and 394 (night)

East Witton

Map Ref: 87SE1485

The A6108 from Masham to Leyburn makes a sharp turn at East Witton, by-passing most of the village but allowing a tantalising glimpse of a long, sloping green flanked by unassuming stone cottages. A closer view shows a similarity between the houses, but no planned uniformity, although it is obviously an estate village. The Earl of Ailesbury, whose family had acquired the former Jervaulx Abbey estate two centuries previously, rebuilt most of East Witton in the early years of last century, the houses and gardens occupying precisely the same positions as they had done in 1627, according to an old estate map. Five small cottages on the green were removed, and a group of six at the top of the green reduced to two. To the east of the village the church was rebuilt on a new site by the road, in 1809, replacing the old church of St Martin whose site to the south-east is now embowered in trees.

East Witton lay at the edge of Jervaulx Abbey park, and, with Coverdale to the west, was well-suited for a market, acquiring a charter in 1307, which eventually died out in the 18th century. Jervaulx Abbey, 1½ miles to the east, was one of Yorkshire's great Cistercian monasteries, founded in 1156 and owning large estates, particularly in upper Wensleydale. Today, the ruins are in private ownership, but open to the public (honesty-box). There is a free car park opposite the entrance. Exquisitely situated in a parkland setting the ruins are famous less for their architecture than for the wild flowers that grow all over them in a calm, informal beauty unruled either by herbicides, geometric paths, or the need for manicured lawns.

A very narrow road continues westwards through East Witton to Coverham, passing Braithwaite Hall, a large mid-17th-century hall now owned by the National Trust but used as a working farmhouse. It has a stone-flagged hall, some fine 18th-century panelling and staircase, and has been tastefully furnished. It can be visited by prior arrangement with the tenants, Mr & Mrs D Duffus. (Wensleydale 40287).

A line of houses called The Street is Garsdale's only community

Garsdale

Map Ref: SD7992 to SD6791

The only main road through the heart of the dales, A684, is a scenic east-west route linking the A1 near Bedale with the M6 near Kendal. It runs through Wensleydale from Leyburn to the valley-head, crosses the Pennine watershed at Garsdale Head, and continues through Garsdale to Sedbergh. Garsdale itself is a narrow green valley extending about ten miles westwards from Garsdale Head, between the steep flanks of Baugh Fell and Rise Hill, both now darkened with the conifers of private afforestation. Names of farms by the roadside or dotted along the lower slopes of the hills reflect Norse origins – Knudmaning, Dandra Garth, Thursgill and Raygill, birthplace in 1734 of John Dawson, who became an apothecary, a surgeon and eventually a famous mathematician. Becks tumble down steep courses from the fells, augmenting the quick, brown waters of the River Clough where trout glide in shady pools.

Garsdale is a valley of bridges, single-arched structures of stone built in the late 18th and early 19th centuries when the road was turnpiked, to link it with the farms and houses on the opposite side of the river. Some of Garsdale's houses are three-storeyed, more often only two, usually with narrower window-spans than elsewhere in the dales as a result of the poorer quality of local stone. White-washed fronts are commonplace, and a few date-panels survive.

Half way down the valley is its only community, consisting of a few houses, cottages, farms, church (rebuilt 1861), chapel (1841), post office, shop, school and garage. Collectively known as The Street this is where the dale changes and widens, with more 'bottom' land becoming apparent. Stone walls of the upper dale give way to hedges, with a marked softening of the austerity. Three miles beyond The Street the road crosses an open stretch of Longstone Fell with panoramic views of the Howgill Fells, appreciated from a large roadside car park. Below, at Garsdale Foot, and spanned by Danny Bridge, the River Clough surges through a ravine of limestone and slate before entering its final couple of miles which take it to the River Rawthey above Sedbergh.

AA recommends:
Self Catering: Railway Cottage, *tel.* Blackpool 28936 (am) and 43471 (pm)

Drove Roads

The droving trade, particularly of cattle from Scotland, flourished for almost 200 years from the end of the 17th century. Huge numbers of beasts, up to 200 at a time, in the charge of a drover helped by a boy and a couple of dogs, walked steadily southwards to the great English markets of the Midlands and the south at 10–12 miles a day, along quiet, un-turnpiked roads, avoiding villages and cultivated land, crossing rivers and streams by fords. The drovers favoured wide open tracks and lanes, travelled rough and slept rough, occasionally enjoying a livelier night at a drovers' inn such as that at Gearstones, near Ribble Head. Small paddocks or wayside stances provided overnight grazing for the beasts.

Drovers' roads entered the Yorkshire Dales at Tan Hill, coming down Arkengarthdale, crossing Reeth Moor into Swaledale at Feetham, over to Askrigg, then by the Roman road over Cam Fell into Ribblesdale and Settle, or branching to Malham. An alternative route from Askrigg crossed the Stake Pass to Buckden in Wharfedale, Littondale and Malham. The 'high way' above Mallerstang into Garsdale and across to Dentdale joined the Craven Way along Whernside's northern shoulder before descending to Chapel-le-Dale and linking with the Ribblesdale route. Some of these old ways are still lonely moorland tracks, others have become metalled roads so that it is hard to realise that around 1745 as many as 10,000 cattle were moving along the drove roads at any one time. Great Close on Malham Moor is still an enormous field north-east of the Tarn. In the 18th century its 732 acres were used for pasturing Scottish cattle, and in one summer 20,000 beasts grazed there.

By the mid-19th century the de-creased demand for Scottish cattle and the development of the railways contributed to a steady decline in droving and the trade virtually ended by the turn of the century.

An old drove road to Askrigg in Wensleydale

Gayle

Map Ref: 84SD8789

Now forming part of the parish of Hawes in Wensleydale and almost linked to the market-town, Gayle is the older community. The village lies at the foot of Sleddale, close-clustered on both sides of Duerley Beck whose course determined its setting and its shape. Beds of limestone form shelves over which the water flows and falls, fordable at the top of the village when the water is low, bridged lower down to carry

Gayle's Old Hall has a carved door head composed of three initials and a date

the minor road to upper Wharfedale, which climbs out of Sleddale on to Fleet Moss, at 1934 feet the highest road in North Yorkshire.

Gayle's narrow alleys, some cobbled, have delightful names – Beckstones, Marridales, Hargill, Wynd, Gaits and Thundering Lane. Near the bridge Old Hall has an elaborately carved door-head dated 1695, but the village is predominantly one of cottages, although a few Georgian frontages add a touch of ostentation. Knitting survived as a cottage industry in Gayle more than anywhere else in Wensleydale. About 1784 a cotton-mill was built by the beck, below the bridge, but soon changed to spinning wool for yarn, helping Gayle to become a centre for the knit hosiery trade, but the mill ceased about 1850, became a saw mill and is now a joiners' shop. Tall houses on the Beckstones were formerly combing-houses for the mill.

Giggleswick

Map Ref: 94SD8063

The busy A65 crosses the River Ribble at Settle and just touches Giggleswick, leaving the village in relative peace to be explored leisurely on foot. In medieval times it was part of the extensive Percy properties in the north of England, and its church, dedicated to St Alkelda, dates from the 12th century, although most of the building is 15th-century work. Its long, low profile with no interior division between nave and chancel, is a characteristic style of Craven churches. Seventeenth-century woodwork includes pulpit, lectern, communion rails and almsbox, and a monument of 1841 commemorates Dr George Birkbeck, who was born in Settle and founded the Mechanics' Institutes which proliferated in industrial villages and towns from the 1820s.

Near the church are some fine late 17th-century houses of pale, local limestone, with drip-mouldings and mullioned windows. Colourwash is used to protect this rather porous building-material. Friendly ducks enjoy the clear waters of Tems Beck, spanned by a single slate slab almost 12 feet across. A beckside path leads to more attractive cottage-groups and the splendid 18th-century Beck House, now two houses, but all the while the scene is dominated by the landmark of the greened copper dome of the chapel of Giggleswick

Giggleswick's most attractive 17th-century houses lie near the church

School. This famous northern boys' school, founded as a chantry school, was given a royal charter in 1553, and its present buildings west of the village show the Victorian Tudor preferences. The chapel, designed in 1897, was completed in 1901.

AA recommends:
Guesthouses: Woodlands, The Mains, *tel.* Settle 2576
Close House (farmhouse), *tel.* Settle 3540

Grassington

Map Ref: 96SE0064

Some dales' villages have the importance and character, if not the status, of towns, each serving as a metropolis for its own valley. Grassington fulfils this function for Wharfedale, yet retains its friendly village atmosphere. Historically important Wharfedale roads meet nearby, the B6265 Skipton-Pateley Bridge road, and the B6160 from Ilkley up Wharfedale to Buckden and beyond. Additionally, the monastic route from Malham to Fountains Abbey passed through Grassington, so it is easy to appreciate why it developed.

Bronze and Iron Age settlement at Lea Green, north of the village, suggest an early favourable site, but the present Grassington is an Anglian settlement which, after the Conquest, passed through the manorial ownership of Percys, Plumptons and Cliffords before descending to the Dukes of Devonshire. In 1282 it was granted a charter for a weekly market and an annual fair, and these continued until the 19th century. Change in land use from the early 17th century, when lead-mining began to assume more importance, brought some prosperity, reflected in the building of many houses in the later part of that century.

But Grassington's heyday came during the late 18th and early 19th centuries, following new developments by the Dukes of Devonshire in lead-mining on Grassington Moor, and the building of the turnpike roads. From 1790 the local textile industry expanded through taking over waterpowered former corn-mills, but when steam-power replaced water-power later last century the mills closed. At the same time lead-mining declined, but the opening of the Yorkshire Dales Railway to Threshfield in 1901 brought new visitors, many of whom settled, perhaps finding work in Skipton or in the developing limestone quarries. Today Grassington is the main residential and tourist centre in upper Wharfedale, superbly situated, with good shops and other amenities, including car-parking, with the main one adjoining the offices of the Yorkshire Dales National Park. Unusually, however, Grassington possesses no Anglican church, but

Grassington Town Trail

Start at the bottom of Market Square, partially cobbled, and the heart of the village. Immediately on the west side is Church House, mainly 17th century (datestone 1694) with Georgian windows above. On the opposite side is Grassington House, splendidly 1760, all symmetry and tall sash windows. Below this, on the east side is Pletts Fold, one of many small, compact groups representing 17th- and 18th-century infilling of crofts belonging to individual houses, built up as the village expanded. Beyond Grassington House and the Black Horse Inn, a former coaching inn, is the Upper Wharfedale Museum. Garrs Lane leaves the top of the square on the right, Main Street leading to Moor Road, on the left. The Congregational Church of 1812 is near the top of Garrs Lane, with Theatre Cottage, converted from a barn and used last century as a theatre. Beyond it to the left is Pletts Barn, now converted, but still showing its remarkable 17th-century character, with arched ventilation slits and pigeon-holes. Near the top of Main Street, which widens into a car park, is the Town Hall built in 1885 as the Mechanics Institute, now the Devonshire Institute.

Upper Wharfedale Museum, Grassington

Chapel Street leads to the north-west, with more 'folds'. Seventeenth-century Town Head Farm at the end is its best building, contrasting with 19th-century miners' cottages on the way. Swinging left and left again, Garrs End Lane leads back to Main Street, passing Ranters' Fold and Chamber End Fold, where the end house facing the small square is a handsome 17th-century building with later window changes, but retaining its stepped, three-light window in the top storey – these small tripartite windows are a feature of houses in this part of Wharfedale. To explore fully every little alley and fold which give Grassington so much character and charm is a rewarding journey into the past and deserves at least an hour.

---

has always shared the beautiful 12th-century church at Linton on the opposite side of the river, with the three nearby townships of Linton, Threshfield and Hebden. Grassington has a lively Arts Festival in June and an Artists' Exhibition in August.

AA recommends:
Hotels: Grassington House,
5 The Square, 1-star,
tel. Grassington 752406
Self Catering: Jerry and Bens,
tel. Grassington 752369 (1½ miles E on B6265 at Hebden)
Guesthouses: Ashfield House Hotel,
tel. Grassington 752584
Garages: Grassington Service Station,
Station Road, *tel.* Grassington 752202

Greenhow Hill

Map Ref: 97SE1164

Few villages occupy so bleak and exposed a situation as Greenhow Hill, on the B6265 between Grassington and Pateley Bridge. At 1300 feet it is one of Yorkshire's highest villages, developed solely as a lead-mining community from the early 17th century. Lead-ore had been mined at Greenhow in Roman times, but the industry did not reach its peak until the 18th and 19th centuries.

The scattered settlement, straggling along the road, is loosely centred on The Miners' Arms, but its characteristic feature is the evidence of a dual economy. Numerous small, isolated cottages, each with its croft of land, and reached along narrow walled lanes, represent homes of former lead-miners who kept oxen and horses for working in the mines. A few other livestock would also have been kept, so that the tiny income from a smallholding and croft might supplement money earned in the mine. Old levels, workings and ruined smelt-mills survive on the moors and in the little valleys to the north of the road. Stone-quarrying and the recovery of fluorspar from old spoil-heaps maintain an air of industrial activity about Greenhow Hill, but lead-mining ceased by the end of last century, and miners' cottages have become holiday homes.

Greenhow Hill is just outside the National Park, but within the Park boundary to the west is Stump Cross Caverns, a magnificent cave system discovered by lead-miners in 1858. The main cave has been developed into an impressive show cave, floodlit to show visitors the splendid stalactite and stalagmite formations.

Greenhow Hill, one of Yorkshire's most remote villages, is composed of isolated cottages like the one shown here

Grinton

Map Ref: 86SE0498

Eleven miles west of Richmond the Swaledale road, B6270, crosses the river at Grinton, leaving the gentler sylvan landscape of the lower dale for the wilder scenery and higher skylines to the west. Most of Grinton's grey stone houses and cottages straggle along the road to the south of the church or up the steep hill that climbs to the heather moors where two upland roads cross into Wensleydale. St Andrew's was the mother-church for the whole of upper Swaledale until Tudor times, and to its churchyard came burials from remote farms and hamlets over a dozen miles away. Fragments of the original Norman church survive but the long, low, broad building is largely 15th century.

Gunnerside is full of melancholy beauty. Meadows are dotted with lonely barns

Grinton's fair was held on Sundays for churchgoers who travelled from afar

A narrow road leads westwards to Harkerside, on the south side of Swaledale, passing some open common where junipers thrive, and there are fine views up the dale. On the moors above are prehistoric earthworks and the more numerous remains of large-scale lead-mining activity of two centuries ago, including, by Cogden Gill, an early 19th-century smelt-mill. Grinton Lodge, on the moor-edge, is a 19th-century battlemented shooting-lodge, used since the 1940s as a Youth Hostel.

Gunnerside

Map Ref: 85SD9598

Swaledale's austere, majestic, if sometimes melancholy beauty seems to crowd in at Gunnerside. The road from Reeth, B6270, along the north side of the valley, makes a sharp turn and crosses the Swale on a sloping bridge, to continue up the dale on the south side, a route taken only since about 1830. Before then it had kept to the north, along the route of the old Corpse Way. Norse settlers chose well this site by Gunnerside Beck, at the foot of sheltering hills to the north. Seen today from above the bridge, or better still from the road to Crackpot, Gunnerside is seen really to nestle, the meadows between it and the river are patterned with stone walls, dotted with hay-barns.

Gunnerside claims no architectural merit, no prettiness, no charm, yet it exudes the spirit of Swaledale. Stone from its huddled houses came from the fells above; dark, damp workings in the hills yielded the lead which enabled Gunnerside to prosper, and when the industry ended towards the close of last century the village too declined. But between the wars and in more recent years it has become increasingly popular with visitors, and former lead-miners' houses have been restored as holiday cottages.

Behind the village Gunnerside Gill cleaves its dramatic gorge between steep-sided fells, and nowhere in the dales are the scars and ruins of lead-mining seen in a setting of such wild beauty. A small car park by the former Miners' Institute is an encouragement to explore on foot (signposted and way-marked path) the east side of Gunnerside Gill. For almost four miles a good track can be followed to the lonely heart of the hills, by the beck or higher up, past spoil heaps, ruined buildings, the small-arched entrance to old levels, and, most impressive of all, the savage hillside gashes caused by repeated 'hushings' in search of the valuable grey ore. A return can be made at a higher level along the eastern hillside, or by a good but tedious track on the west side of Gunnerside Gill.

Hawes

Map Ref: 84SD8789

Most market towns in the Yorkshire Dales are at the lower end of the valleys they serve. Hawes is different, being near the head of Wensleydale, 850 feet above sea-level, with high fells to both north and south sweeping up 1000 feet beyond that. It is also a relative newcomer, receiving its Market Charter as recently as 1700, a recognition of the growth of its trade, mainly by packhorse traffic, in the previous century. No record exists of a settlement here until 1307 when, in the Forest of Wensleydale, it was Le Thouse, a pass through the hills.

Today, the A684 passes through the small town (population 1000) above the southern bank of the River Ure, on its way from Leyburn to Sedbergh. Lesser roads lead north and south to the neighbouring valleys of Swaledale and Wharfedale, while the B6255 crosses into Ribblesdale on the route of the Richmond-Lancaster turnpike which came through Hawes in 1795. From the Moorcock Inn a few miles westwards, the B6259 branches northwards through Mallerstang to

Kirkby Stephen and the Vale of Eden. Thus, Hawes benefits from its position at the centre of good road communications as it also enjoyed a boom in the 1870s when the railway line came up the dale and was linked to the Settle-Carlisle line at Hawes Junction, later renamed Garsdale. The railway stimulated local trade and industry, particularly quarrying and dairying. Although many of the buildings of Hawes date from late Victorian times they are interspersed in the Market Place area and near the old bridge with houses of the 17th and 18th centuries.

Hawes is now the commercial and market centre of upper Wensleydale, with a good range of shops, hotels, guesthouses and holiday cottages, as well as camping and caravanning sites, and a popular Youth Hostel, reflecting its growing importance as a touring centre for visitors. Hawes' shops are small, independent family concerns offering good-quality goods, many of them made locally, and the good service at them and at the market stalls contributes to Hawes' reputation as a friendly market town.

Hawes Auction Mart is one of the most important livestock markets in the district; the Wensleydale Creameries in Gayle Lane (not open to visitors) is the 'home' of the famous Wensleydale Cheese; there is a National Park Information Centre in the former railway station, and an adjacent large car park (charge); the former engine shed nearby now houses the impressive Upper Dales Folk Museum, and near the entrance to the car park is the remarkable Hawes Ropeworks, where visitors can see ropes being made. Many rope products are for sale as are other craft goods.

Aspects of Hawes – Top: A 19th-century 'nodding head' toy in the Upper Dales Folk Museum. Left: Hawes Ropeworks. Right: The famous livestock market

AA recommends:

Hotels: Fountain, Market Place, 2-star, *tel.* Hawes 206
Simonstone Hall Hotel, 2-star, *tel.* Hawes 255
Campsites: Bainbridge Ings Caravan and Camping Site, 2-pennants, *tel.* Hawes 354
Self Catering: Beckside and Dyers Cottages, Dyers Garth, *tel.* Blackpool 28936 (day) and 43471 (evenings)
Brunskill Cottage, *tel.* Hawes 359
Dalesway Cottage, Gayle Road, *tel.* Blackpool 28936 (day) and 43471 (evening)
High Shaw Farmhouse, *tel.* Hawes 359
Mirk Pot Farmhouse, *tel.* Hawes 303 or York 20910
West Cottage, *tel.* Hawes 303 or York 20910

Hawes Town Trail

Start at the National Park car park near the small roundabout at the eastern end of the one-way system. Follow the one-way street into the town, passing first the Post Office, originally the grammar-school of 1729. Cross Gayle Beck by Hawes Bridge. Upstream on the right is the former building of the Wensleydale Cheese Factory, downstream on the left the old building was formerly Hawes corn mill. Ahead, on the right of the narrow cobbled section of street, the White Hart was a coaching-inn and staging-post, its busy years between 1795 and the railway era. Opposite and above is Hawes church, rebuilt in 1851, with many unmarked graves in the church-yard, an indication of poverty in late Victorian times.

Bealer Bank is a flagged causeway between the church and Gayle village, which can be followed, returning to Hawes by Gayle Lane, past the Creamery. Continuing from the White Hart into Market Place, the small butcher's shop by the Market Hall was the market toll-house, while the open space beyond the Market Hall, Penny Garth, was formerly used as part of the street auction of cattle and sheep. Beyond Gayle Lane was the 'hearse house', where the parish hearse was kept, but the 1643 date on the house below is misleading! Opposite is the working smithy, and the return journey, along the north side of the Market Place passes Cocketts Hotel, formerly a Quaker

Hawes Fair in 1904

rest house, with an interesting in-scribed, dated lintel, 1668, above an adjoining doorway. Set back beyond it is Rose House, 1692, one of the best surviving 17th-century houses in the town. Barclays' Bank building dates from 1889, re-fronted in 1920. North of the roundabout, by the Hardraw road, is the Quaker Burial Ground, given to the Friends in 1680.

Hubberholme Church, a place of beauty and tranquillity, is further distinguished by the delightful carved mice within, the 'signature' of craftsman Robert Thompson

Horton in Ribblesdale

Map Ref: 90SD8072

The road from Settle to Hawes, B6479, follows the River Ribble for ten miles to its source near Ribble Head, where it joins the B6255 from Ingleton. Horton is about the mid-point, an ideal centre for exploring limestone landscapes, green hillsides, woods and caves of upper Ribblesdale. The village stretches for half a mile along the road from the corner by the church and the Golden Lion to the bridges by the New Inn, near which is a free car park, with toilets.

Horton's houses illustrate developments in the dale. Yeomen's farmhouses of the late 17th century are at the edge of the village, especially on its eastern side. Near the churchyard and the New Inn are later cottages, while Victorian terraces reflect the coming of the railway in the 1870s. More recent are the villas and quarrymen's houses built when the limestone quarries first scarred the slopes of Moughton, west of the railway, about 1890, and which have greatly expanded since the last war.

Eastwards, however, the view is serene and challenging, dominated by the proud, stepped profile of Pen-y-ghent (2277 feet), one of the famous 'Three Peaks' of upper Ribblesdale, its summit about three miles from the village, reached by the Pennine Way track along Horton Scar Lane, which passes close to Hull Pot and Hunt Pot on the way. Horton is one of the most popular stopping-places for Pennine Way walkers, whose subsequent route northwards follows old tracks along the eastern side of Ribblesdale to High Birkwith and Cam High Road. 'Three Peaks' challengers also like Horton as a starting and finishing-point. These and other visitors will appreciate the calm benediction of St Oswald's church, grey-stoned, squat-towered, with Norman doorway and nave arcades. Lychgates to its churchyard are roofed with huge slabs of the ancient Horton slates.

AA recommends:
Guesthouses: Crown Hotel (inn), *tel.* Horton in Ribblesdale 209

The Howgill Fells

Map Ref: 82SD6798

When the Yorkshire Dales National Park was designated in 1954 the former county boundary between Yorkshire and Westmorland bisected the Howgill Fells in an east-west line. Bureaucratic tidiness incorporated the Yorkshire half within the National Park. This, together with the whole north-western sector of the National Park, is now in Cumbria but still lies within the Yorkshire Dales National Park, so merits reference here.

The Howgills comprise about 40 square miles of green, rounded, lonely hills, smooth-sided, beautiful, and uninterrupted by walls, hedges, or fences above the intakes. To their open, grassy uplands, reaching above 2000 feet, there is unrestricted access, and walkers' rewards are of widespread, panoramic views, especially from the southern and western borders.

Valley roads clearly define the boundaries of the Howgills – A684 through Sedbergh on the south, M6 or A685 in the Lune gorge to the west, A685 along the upper Lune along the north, and A683 in the Rawthey valley down the eastern side. Sedbergh, Tebay and Ravenstonedale are at the points of the Howgills' triangular plan. Walks on to the fells are most easily done from Sedbergh, Howgill Lane – a very narrow, scenic road from Sedbergh to Low Borrowbridge in the Lune gorge, and from Cautley in the Rawthey valley. But it is the long, remote valleys which penetrate from their northern flanks which reveal to the discerning explorer the secret, hidden places of these lovely hills.

Hubberholme

Map Ref: 91SD9278

The road up Wharfedale, B6160, divides at Buckden, the main route climbing over Kidstones Pass into Bishopdale and Wensleydale, leaving a minor, narrow road to continue into the wild beauty of upper Wharfedale. In a mile it passes the hamlet of Hubberholme whose church, dedicated to St Michael and All Angels, is now the parish church for the upper dale, but originated as a Forest chapel, and after the Dissolution of Monasteries was served by curates from Arncliffe in Littondale.

For thousands of visitors it is a place of pilgrimage, probably the best-loved of all Dales churches. Its superb riverside setting, against a backcloth of wooded hillside and distant bare fells, is a perfect frame for its broad, low profile and short, sturdy tower. The interior is memorable, with unplastered walls of rough local stone contributing to a remarkably medieval atmosphere, enhanced by the rare survival of an exquisite rood-loft of 1558, one of only two in Yorkshire. Carved in oak, painted red, black and gold, it is contemporary with much of the building including the windows and the tower. A modern window in the south aisle is a visual story of the parish, although it does not illustrate the time when the river flooded into the church, and as its level receded fish were seen swimming in the nave. The church was sympathetically repaired in 1863, when the walls were stripped, and again in 1955–56. Almost all the woodwork is modern oak, made by Robert Thompson of Kilburn in 1934, and his signature, a tiny church mouse, can be identified on many of the pieces, usually hidden away in inconspicuous places.

The George Inn by the roadside was originally the vicarage, but remained church property even as an inn until 1965. Here, on each New Year's Day, is the ceremony of letting the 'Poor Pasture', a custom almost 1000 years old, when farmers bid for the tenancy of a 16-acre field behind the inn which had been left in trust for the poor of the parish. The vicar used to perform the auction, but this is now done by a local auctioneer. Proceeds from it go to help old people in the parish. Between the inn and the church Hubberholme bridge was on an old and important route between Lancaster and Newcastle, noted as being in decay in 1639, ruined in 1709 and rebuilt in 1734.

AA recommends:

Hotels: Buck Inn, Buckden, 1-star,
tel. Kettlewell 227

Guesthouses: George (inn), Kirk Gill,
tel. Kettlewell 223

Ingleton

Map Ref: 88SD6973

When the railway line came from
Settle in 1849, and the dominating
viaduct helped to extend it to
Sedbergh ten years later, Victorian
train-borne travellers began to put
Ingleton on the tourist map. Today,
the A65 following the route of the
Keighley-Kendal turnpike of 1753,
brings the motorist, although the
main road now just by-passes the
village. Lancaster is only 18 miles
away by the A687, with Hawes the
same distance to the north-east along
the B6255. Good car parking
facilities near the Community Centre
encourage a stay and some
exploration.

Village streets are narrow and
winding, centred on a tiny market
place. Nearby the late Victorian
church has one of the finest Norman

*Ingleborough's 2372ft-bulk shelters
Ingleton, where White Scar Caves and
the falls attract visitors*

fonts in Yorkshire. Bell Horse Gate
descends steeply to the river whose
water once worked mills, but these
are now derelict, although their mill-
worker's cottages form neat terraces
almost in the shadow of the viaduct.
Wool and cotton-spinning were an
important local industry in the 18th
and 19th centuries.

As long ago as 1884 a group of
residents, recognising tourist
potential in the local scenery, formed
the Ingleton Improvement Society,
and over the next thirty years created
miles of paths, built steps and bridges
along the increasingly popular walks
up the valleys of the Doe and Twiss,
which, probably because the word
sounds more romantic, were called
glens. The 'Falls Walk' (charge) is
today Ingleton's best-known
attraction, with a small car park near
the entrance. On the Hawes road, a
mile outside the village, White Scar
Caves are another of Ingleton's
special attractions, and are open
daily.

Ingleborough (2372 feet) is the
best-known, if not quite the highest,

of Yorkshire's Three Peaks, its
limestone-stepped bulk sheltering
Ingleton on the north-east, a familiar
and perpetual challenge. The ascent
from Ingleton via Fell Lane and
Crina Bottom is relatively easy,
though rather tedious, with a steep
climax to the summit plateau, once
the site of a huge Iron Age fort.

Limestone quarrying has created
unsightly scars above the village, but
vanished now are the remains of
Ingleton's coal-mine south of the
village. Although mining is but a
memory the brick-built miners'
houses of 1913–14 form an
interesting 'new village' on Ingleton's
eastern edge.

AA recommends:

Guesthouses: Oakroyd Private Hotel,
Main Street, *tel.* Ingleton 41258
Springfield Private Hotel, Main Street,
tel. Ingleton 41280
Langber (farmhouse), *tel.* Ingleton 41587

Early Visitors to the Dales

The Dales have attracted visitors
for over 250 years, although
the earliest written accounts of
visits go back to Tudor times, with
John Leland about 1546 and the
historian Camden in 1582. In the 17th
century the northern dales played an
important part in the founding of
Quakerism, and George Fox's
preaching travels through the area are
recorded in his Journal of 1652.

Celia Fiennes rode side-saddle
through England in the 1690s, including
Richmond in her itinerary, and finding
it a 'sad shatter'd town much to
Decay', while in 1724 Defoe's travels
brought him to Skipton and Settle
from where he saw to the north-west
'high mountains which had a terrible
aspect . . . especially Penigent.'
However, he did reach Burnsall and
Richmond. Fifty years later John
Wesley's Journals refer to successful

*George Fox 'saw the light' in 1652, then
travelled the Dales preaching Quakerism*

meetings at Redmire, Wensley and
Richmond, and six years on, at Grassington and Pateley Bridge.

Tourists, an early 19th-century
word meaning people with sufficient

wealth and leisure to travel primarily
for pleasure, began to penetrate the
Dales from about 1750 onwards, encouraged by improved roads. Bishop
Pococke in 1751 was impressed with
Wensleydale; in 1773 Thomas
Pennant, en route to Scotland, found
good hospitality in Settle, while 20
years later, the Hon. John Byng (later
Lord Torrington) tended to find more
to criticise than to praise, being dis-
tinctly upset by the new noisy cotton-
mill by Aysgarth Force. Thomas Gray
was horrified at Gordale Scar's
frowning crags in 1769, and in
October 1802 Wordsworth and his
new bride Mary, with sister Dorothy
naturally present, travelled up
Wensleydale on their honeymoon
journey from Brompton, near
Scarborough. They changed horses at
Aysgarth, walked to the falls and
stayed overnight at Hawes before
continuing to Grasmere. Dorothy's
Journal records the favourable
impressions they all felt.

Keld

Map Ref: 79NY8901

Green hills enfold this tiny grey stone village at the head of Swaledale, 22 miles from Richmond by one of England's most scenic roads. The final switchback stretch to Keld is above a dry valley, the river's course having taken it round the eastern side of Kisdon's isolated hill. Cottages cluster close around a tiny square above the river, and one road ends there, with space for only a handful of cars. Two chapels, the school and the gaunt Youth Hostel at Keld Green, are the biggest buildings in this remote place.

The riverside scenery is superb, with the Swale sweeping into a wooded limestone gorge below the village, and crossed by a footbridge carrying the Pennine Way en route for the Tan Hill Inn four moorland miles away. An easy walk above the north side of the wooded gorge leads to Crackpot Hall (a ruined farm) and the dramatic ravine of Swinnergill. The Pennine Way enters the village by a high-level route round Kisdon's eastern and northern shoulder. The much older Corpse Way crosses its windy plateau.

Above Keld, a lonely road heads westwards into the wilderness landscape of upper Swaledale and crosses to Kirkby Stephen. A mile along it a branch heads northwards, over Park Bridge, up a double-hairpin hill to West Stonesdale and Tan Hill Inn. All around is the austere grandeur of high Pennine fells, a landscape of wide horizons and splendid solitude.

Fishermen at Kilnsey trout farm don't tell tall stories – the fish really are big!

Keld is surrounded by soaring green fells punctuated by isolated barns

Kettlewell

Map Ref: 92SD9772

In the 12th century, part of Kettlewell's manor was granted to the canons of Coverham Abbey across the hills to the north. Fountains Abbey and Bolton Priory also had estates here, so it was natural that a market was established in the 13th century, and the village became a thriving community. Textiles, and, in the late 18th and early 19th centuries, lead-mining, revitalised village prosperity and Kettlewell's appearance today derives much from the past 200 years. The remains of the smelting-mill, used from 1700 to 1886, can be seen near the confluence of Cam and Dowber Becks half a mile above the village.

The B6160, coming up Wharfedale from Threshfield, crosses the Wharfe into Kettlewell by a handsome stone bridge, and there is a good riverside car park immediately beyond this. Three inns – the Racehorses, the Blue Bell and the King's Head – testify to Kettlewell's popularity with visitors, and in addition there are numerous guesthouses and holiday cottages.

The main road touches only the southern edge of the village, and a stroll through its quiet lanes and turnings reveals a number of 17th- and 18th-century houses, including the vicarage. The church, however, is late Victorian. Apart from its beautiful setting Kettlewell's main appeal is as a base from which to explore the surrounding landscapes, along inviting riverside paths above and below the bridge, by steeper, rougher tracks up Dowber Gill as an approach to Great Whernside (2308 feet), to Starbotton by woodland paths or the exciting green lane of Top Mere Road, or, for the energetic, a climb over the tops to Arncliffe or Hawkswick in Littondale. The minor road to Conistone down Wharfedale's eastern side passes Scargill House, a Church of England conference and

holiday centre with a church built in Scandinavian style. Coniferous plantations contrast with the paler greens of deciduous woodland, and gleaming limestone scars etch the hillsides while valley fields display the planned geometry of late 18th-century enclosure, punctuated with stone barns.

AA recommends:

Hotels: Racehorses, 2-star, *tel.* Kettlewell 233
Blue Bell, Middle Lane, 1-star, *tel.* Kettlewell 230
Self Catering: Maypole Cottage, *tel.* Kettlewell 202
Guesthouses: Dale House, *tel.* Kettlewell 836

Kilnsey

Map Ref: 96SD9767

Wharfedale's outstanding landscape feature is Kilnsey Crag, a gigantic thrust of the Great Scar Limestone towering 170 feet above the B6160 four miles above Grassington. A remarkable 40-feet overhang at the top has presented rock-climbers with one of their stiffest challenges. Earth-bound mortals merely gaze in awe. During the later stages of the Ice Age the Wharfedale glacier scoured back the recessed base of the cliff, where springs gush out and form a roadside beck.

Kilnsey itself is a handful of houses and the Tennant Arms Hotel. Behind, by the road which marks the beginning of Mastiles Lane, is Kilnsey Old Hall, built in 1648 on the site of a busy grange of Fountains Abbey. The Hall is now used as a farm store, retains its outside stone stair, and by the courtyard entrance survives part of the 15th-century gatehouse of the grange. Mastiles Lane was a monastic track, now a green lane, leading to monastic estates on Malham Moor, and beyond the Ribble, to the Lake District.

Nearby, Kilnsey Park has been developed as a Visitor Centre orientated towards freshwater fish. There are specially-designed trout-fishing lakes and a trout-feeding pond. In the farm shop fresh trout, smoked trout, pheasants, ducks, and rabbits can be bought, as well as cold-water tropical fish. A 'Riverlife Museum' displays in a well-designed series of aquaria a fine variety of British freshwater fish, and upstairs visual exhibits and audio-visual presentations illustrate many aspects of wildlife in the Dales.

Along more traditional lines Kilnsey Show, first held in 1897, is one of Wharfedale's most popular annual events, taking place on August Bank Holiday Tuesday. Livestock displays, sheepdog-trials, rural crafts, flat races, galloping and horse-trotting, and the Crag Race, provide a series of exciting, competitive events.

Langcliffe

Map Ref: 94SD8265

From Settle the B6479 road up Ribblesdale misses most of Langcliffe, which as a result enjoys a seclusion unusual among Dales villages. Informal rows of stone cottages keep their distance round a spacious green, most colourful in late October with a golden canopy of beeches. The village once belonged to Sawley Abbey in lower Ribblesdale, but in more recent times depended on its cotton-mill, now used as a paper-mill. Although a few houses have 17th-century datestones most suggest by their appearance that Langcliffe was a no-nonsense industrial community from the late 18th century.

A narrow road climbs steeply north-eastwards and crosses the uplands to Malham about seven miles away. Near the crest of the hill a good track leads to Victoria Cave, where discoveries of bones, flints and tools indicate cave occupation to 9000 BC. Further south are the fine limestone cliffs of Attermire Scar.

Langstrothdale

Map Ref: SD8780 to SD9278

Above Buckden the upper valley of the Wharfe is known as

Yockenthwaite, a Norse–Irish name for the 'clearing of Eogan', has a stone circle

Langstrothdale. Founded in Norman times Langstrothdale Chase was formerly a hunting preserve for deer and game, having its own Forest laws, courts, privileges and punishments. Settled in Norse times a thousand years ago by people coming from the west and north, its Norse sheep farms became lodges in the Forest, and these survive today as the hamlet-settlements in the valley – Cray, Hubberholme, Raisgill, Yockenthwaite, Deepdale, Beckermonds and Oughtershaw.

Natural woodland diminishes beyond Yockenthwaite, the valley narrows and becomes wilder. The minor road from Buckden is unfenced here, with sheep-cropped sward on both sides for a while, and the river always close, following a course which takes it over limestone beds and ledges, where it forms weirs and small brown pools. Above Yockenthwaite, hidden behind a wall in a field across the river, is one of the few Bronze Age stone circles in the Dales, with twenty stones forming a rough circle 25 feet across.

The road crosses the river at Deepdale by an iron bridge of 1907 which replaced a stone packhorse structure. At Beckermonds the road divides, its northern arm climbing first to Oughtershaw at 1200 feet, and then to the watershed on Fleet Moss, 1934 feet, the highest road in North Yorkshire, before descending to Wensleydale at Hawes. From Beckermonds the other fork continues westwards through new private afforestation to High Greenfield, where the metalled surface ends. Greenfield was a Fountains Abbey grange so this route probably originated in medieval times. It subsequently formed part of an important packhorse way between Lancaster and Richmond; as a walkers' route today it crosses to Horton in Ribblesdale, joining the Pennine Way on Birkwith Moor.

Date-Panels

'The great rebuilding', as it is often referred to, of houses in England occurred later in the Yorkshire Dales than in most other areas of the country. Apart from the more obvious fortified houses only Friars Head at Winterburn, and possibly West End House in Askrigg are known to pre-date 1600. A few Dales farmhouses were built in Jacobean times, but rebuilding accelerated from the 1630s, peaked towards the end of the century, continued apace until about 1730, when it slowed down. One aspect of this rebuilding is the decorative treatment of doorheads, not only with elaborately carved lintels but with date-panels often incorporated into the design.

Dates on them need to be treated with caution. They may accurately represent the date of a building, or be the date when it was occupied as a marriage-house; they may date an alteration, an addition or an

Top: Datestone in Askrigg's main street
Bottom: Ingman Lodge, Ribblesdale

inheritance. They may not even refer to the building they adorn but have simply been taken from another structure altogether! Almost invariably, however, they are decorative and distinctive. Where only two initials are given they are probably those of the man who built the house. If three initials occur that of the surname usually dominates and is central, the others being the initials of the Christian names of husband and wife. Four initials are uncommon, but would probably represent Christian and surname initials of the pair before marriage.

The most decorative doorheads occur in the Craven area – Wharfedale, Littondale, Ribblesdale – with good examples at Settle. Particularly outstanding is the whole door case at Ingman Lodge, near Selside, whose unusual design incorporates an elegant hood, carved capitals and stone halberds, as well as the date-panel.

Leyburn

Map Ref: 87SE1190

On the important A684 trans-Pennine route between Northallerton and Kendal, which threads much of Wensleydale, Leyburn has developed as the main market, commercial and trading centre for the dale. Yet it is a comparative newcomer, having received its charter only in 1684

Leyburn Shawl reveals a glorious prospect of Wensleydale

when it was a village centred on Grove Square. Many of the buildings which front the large Market Place date from the early years of last century, but the Regency-style Market Hall was not completed until 1856, the same year as the railway arrived from Northallerton and Bedale. Although a single line passes through the town today this merely serves the quarries above Redmire, and there is no passenger traffic.

Leyburn's present appearance is that of a prosperous, late-Georgian market-town, although shop-frontages have largely become anonymously modern. Some 18th-century houses survive, mainly around Grove Square, but the Bolton Arms, at the top of the Market Place, and Leyburn Hall, almost completely hidden behind it, are the best buildings in the town. Unusually, until 1836 Leyburn had no Anglican church.

Townscape becomes landscape very suddenly on Leyburn's western edge. From the top of the Market Place Shawl Terrace leads to an open, grassy terrace on a shelf of limestone. This is the strangely-named Leyburn Shawl, from which a glorious prospect of Wensleydale is revealed, generously-wooded in the near view, with the gently-stepped profile of hills leading the eye into the distance.

With good roads leading northwards to Richmond, south to Middleham, Masham and Ripon, Leyburn is a conveniently-placed tourist centre for lower Wensleydale, and its hotels, holiday cottages and nearby caravan parks cater for an increasing number of visitors.

AA recommends:
Guesthouses: Eastfield Lodge, St Matthews Terrace, *tel.* Wensleydale 23196

Linton

Map Ref: 96SD9962

Situated just off the B6160 on the south side of Wharfedale opposite Grassington, Linton is by any standards one of the outstanding villages in the Yorkshire Dales. Scenically, architecturally, and in

The Dales and the Artist

Perhaps because Art rarely flourishes in an area where climate and environment create harsh living conditions it is not until the relatively easier times of this century that the Dales can claim strong residential associations with artists. However, artists of national repute have found great inspiration in Dales landscapes, led by Girtin. In 1796 he made a lengthy tour of the north and did much sketching around Bolton Abbey, Malham and Richmond, as well as at Greta Bridge and Barnard Castle in Teesdale. Dales scenery between the Wharfe and the Tees features in over thirty water-colours based on these sketches. His work may have influenced Cotman and De Wint, both of whom visited the area, and Constable. It is more than likely that Turner felt encouraged to see the

Dales for himself and travelled to Yorkshire to visit the places which Girtin had painted.

Entering by way of Knaresborough and Ripon he went on to Richmond and Teesdale, continued further north to Northumberland, returning by way of the Lake District and Lancaster to Settle, Skipton and Bolton Abbey. Three Yorkshire scenes were exhibited the next year, 1798, in the Royal Academy. Commissioned work, to illustrate Whitaker's History of Craven and History of Richmondshire brought Turner to Yorkshire again on an extended tour, and he was also asked to paint scenes in Wharfedale and the Craven area for Walter Fawkes of Farnley, near Otley. From

Turner, one of the great masters of landscape art and watercolour, was inspired to paint Semer Water

1808 to 1825 Turner spent part of each summer in the Dales, and produced many paintings and drawings of Wensleydale, Swaledale and Teesdale, Bolton, Barden, Gordale and Ribblesdale, including the caves.

In our own times the artistic tradition has been carried on by painters like Fred Lawson, who came as a young man to Castle Bolton in 1911 and stayed until his death in 1968, and Marie Hartley, E. Charles Simpson, Constance Pearson, Janet Rawlins, Angus Rands, Piers Browne, John Cooke and many other talented artists. Paintings are displayed in many village galleries, annual exhibitions of Dales artists' work is held at Askrigg and Grassington, while the Chandler Gallery, Leyburn and the Linton Court Gallery, Settle, have displays throughout the year, the subjects and/or artists being changed monthly.

terms of its later industrial development, it is full of interest. Sited on well-drained moraine gravels it was attractive to Anglian settlers, and the village pattern originates from those times, with groups of houses informally set around a large irregular green. Linton Beck flows down the middle of the village, crossed by a clapper bridge, a packhorse bridge, a modern road bridge, stepping-stones and fords, and, near the river, Little Emily's Bridge.

Grey stone houses round the green, mainly of 17th- and 18th-century dates, display an unusual dignity, partly explained by the dominating presence of Fountaine Hospital, founded and endowed in 1721 by Richard Fountaine, 'for six poor men or women'. He was timber merchant for Sir John Vanbrugh and it is possible that the great architect may have designed this remarkable structure, far grander than any other building in Wharfedale. Fountaine Hospital introduced the Classical style of building, not only to Wharfedale but to the Dales area in general, its symmetry and Classical motifs were subsequently copied and adapted for Dales houses throughout the rest of the 18th century, usually on a much smaller scale.

At the other end of the green, by the main road, Old Hall shows at its western end typical late 17th-century features, but at the eastern end is a three-storey enlargement of early Georgian times, with a handsome porch and tall sash windows. Nearby is White Abbey (never monastic), a typical 17th-century yeoman's house. 'Beckside', in a fold off the east side of the green, is similarly long and low, with a decorated lintel and datestone of 1642.

Beyond the main road, and half a mile from the village, Linton Church serves the communities of Grassington, Threshfield, Hebden and Linton, each having footpaths leading to it. The late 12th-century building, with its squat bell-turret, shows Norman features, but was largely rebuilt and extended during the 15th century. Until 1866 Linton had two rectors, the result of there having been two Lords of the Manor, each with the right of advowson. On the road to the church, and almost opposite Linton Mill, there is a small car park. The 1850 group of mill-cottages opposite is called Botany, an old West Riding name for houses by a textile mill. The huge mill building, which closed in 1959, dates from 1901–2 when it replaced an earlier one used for spinning worsteds, and after 1840, cotton. Before then a corn-mill utilised the waters of the Wharfe above Linton Falls, where the Tin Bridge carries the church path from Grassington across the river.

Linton's houses, sheltered by trees. The village is broken by a beck

Littondale

Map Ref: SD8776 to SD9769

Charles Kingsley called it Vendale, Wordsworth named it Amerdale and ITV chose it for *Emmerdale Farm*. However, the Ordnance Survey correctly identifies it as Littondale, and the river draining it is the Skirfare. Two minor roads enter the valley from Wharfedale a mile above Kilnsey, one along each side, coming together near Arncliffe and continuing to the valley-head at Halton Gill.

This is Craven country so limestone dominates with scars along green hillsides, bare areas of white rock above Arncliffe, with walls and barns patterning the flat valley floor. Man has found Littondale and its limestone pastures a favoured site since Iron Age times, for the uplands show evidence of early habitations. Anglian settlers utilised well-drained gravel sites for their villages – Arncliffe on the south of the river, Hawkswick, Litton and Halton Gill on the north, nicely spread about 2½ miles apart. In Norman times it was a hunting forest, in medieval days a sheep-rearing estate of Fountains Abbey. After the Dissolution of the Monasteries the pattern of farming changed little – sheep on the hills, cattle in the riverside meadows. Littondale is one of the few valleys in the Dales unscarred by lead-mining.

Most of Littondale's magnificent barns, many with covered porches, date from the time when corn was grown, and carts brought under shelter for unloading it. Large double doors admitted draught to the stone-flagged threshing-floor. Good examples of such barns can be seen in all Littondale villages, but some have been tastefully converted into private residences, especially at Hawkswick and Litton. These small, linear villages contain good houses and cottages of limestone, with roofs of darker flags, whose shallow pitch echo the slopes of the fells beyond. At the head of the dale Halton Gill is a cluster of mainly 17th-century farms and cottages at the foot of Horse Head Pass, an old packhorse route to Raisgill in Langstrothdale.

Riverside paths between Litton, Arncliffe and Hawkswick provide a leisurely way of exploring Littondale, and hill roads out of the valley lead southwards from Arncliffe to Malham or Settle, and from Halton Gill to Stainforth and Ribblesdale. Each traverses the spacious uplands of the Craven limestone; each crosses the line of the Pennine Way, the Halton Gill road passing within a mile of the summit of Pen-y-ghent, the Malham one passing close to Malham Tarn.

Halton Gill in Littondale, a cluster of mainly 17th-century farms and cottages at the foot of Horse Head Pass

Malham

Map Ref: 95SD9062

The nearest main road is six miles to the south. From the A65 between Gargrave and Hellifield minor roads lead northwards, converging at Airton and following the youthful River Aire through Kirkby Malham. The sense of high drama increases as Malham is approached and the great limestone cliff of Malham Cove identified beyond the village. Malham is at a focus of the crescent of Craven's limestone country, where the bare bones of landscape come to the surface in cliffs, crags and scars, and man-made miles of limestone walls impose their disciplined pattern on the land. In stage terms Malham is a 'limestone spectacular', a quality known to tourists for two centuries and recognised by the National Park authority by the creation of a large car park (charge) and excellent Information Centre at the southern entrance to the village. There is virtually no other parking-space in Malham, and none along the roads which climb either side of Malham Cove, or on the way to Gordale Scar. To explore the natural beauties of the area visitors are expected to walk, helped by the many miles of waymarked paths and an invaluable local footpath guide.

Malham Beck, which emerges from the foot of the Cove, flows down a grassy valley and through the centre of the village, spanned by clapper bridges and a former packhorse bridge, now widened. A sloping green forms the village nucleus, with the Lister Arms above, displaying a handsome date-panel, 1723, probably representing a refronting. A stroll around the village reveals many 18th-century datestones on farmhouses and cottages, and there is scarcely a single building which displeases. Trees flourish in this sheltered setting, imparting sylvan overtones to a satisfying harmony of characteristic Dales building. All is stone, mainly limestone, sometimes rendered and whitewashed, sometimes left bare. Mullioned windows are common, and stone roofs universal.

The attractions of the village match the beauty of its surroundings, as a walk along any of the footpaths will reveal. A newly-surfaced stretch of the Pennine Way leads to the Cove, ascending by a steep wooden-framed stair the western grassy side of the 250-feet high cliff, emerging at the top to be confronted by a remarkable limestone pavement with its clints (small flat blocks) and grikes (deep crevices between). The view from the top is sensational and shows, among other things, Celtic fields in the valley. Beyond the top of the Cove the Dry Valley leads northwards towards the Water Sinks and Malham Tarn.

Gordale Scar, a gigantic collapsed cave system between frowning limestone cliffs, is 1½ miles east of Malham, perhaps most scenically reached by a field path by Gordale Beck and Janet's Foss, a charming little waterfall. To Malham's west, Pikedaw Hill is another splendid viewpoint, and much less frequented than the Cove. Twin roads north from Malham join near Malham Tarn, then offer the choice of continuing northwards to Arncliffe or westwards to Ribblesdale.

Malham Tarn is a few hundred yards north of the road, and the Pennine Way passes close to its eastern margin. The 153-acre Tarn forms part of the Malham Tarn estate, owned by the National Trust. It, together with Tarn House, is let to the Field Studies Council who, throughout the year, run a series of short residential courses, mainly for senior pupils from schools and undergraduates, concentrating on biology and geography. Recently introduced holiday courses for adults wishing to learn more about natural history are proving increasingly popular.

Kirkby Malham has the parish church, characteristically long and low-profiled, wholly 15th century, with stone stocks in the churchyard. Good stone houses grace the village street, and a road to the west crosses the moors to Settle.

AA recommends:
Hotels: Buck Inn, 1-star, *tel.* Airton 317
Self Catering: Scalegill, *tel.* Airton 293 (1½ miles S on unclassified road at Kirkby Malham)
Guesthouses: Sparth House Hotel, *tel.* Airton 315
Tudor, *tel.* Airton 301 (4 miles S on unclassified road at Bell Busk)

Mallerstang

Map Ref: SD7992 to NY7708

When the Yorkshire Dales National Park was designated in 1954 the county boundary between Yorkshire and Westmorland (now Cumbria) formed a convenient northern limit at the watershed between the River Ure, quickly turning eastwards into Wensleydale, and the River Eden, flowing northwards towards Kirkby Stephen. Landscapes do not follow bureaucratic lines, and the upper few miles of Wensleydale and the beginnings of Eden tend to form a continuous trough between the Moorcock Inn on the A684 five miles west of Hawes, and Kirkby Stephen ten miles to the north. Beyond the county and National Park boundary the valley is called Mallerstang, one of the few north-south valleys in the northern Pennines, threaded by the B6259.

Austerely beautiful, with scattered farms, a hamlet at Outhgill, and a village at Nateby, Mallerstang is flanked by Wild Boar Fell to the west, Hugh Seat on the east, each well over 2200 feet. Becks tumble down from lonely moorland heights; there are few trees. The Settle-Carlisle railway reaches its summit at Ais Gill, 1169 feet, before making the long, winding descent to Kirkby Stephen. On a grassy knoll above the Eden, where Mallerstang begins to broaden, and limestone features soften the austerity, are the ruins of Pendragon Castle, repeatedly rebuilt – the last time by their owner, Lady Anne Clifford, in 1660. She also rebuilt, three years later, Mallerstang Chapel at Outhgill, as an inscribed stone above its door testifies. Recently, a fine new set of hassocks has been made by local ladies for the chapel, each illustrating some aspect of Mallerstang, its landscape, history, farming and wildlife.

AA recommends:
Self Catering: 1 and 2 Aisgill Moor Cottages, Aisgill, *tel.* Blackpool 28936 (am) and 43471 (pm)

Main picture: Views from Malham Cove's spectacular limestone pavement are superb

inset (left): Malham Tarn is a lake of glacial origin high above sea level

inset (centre): Janet's Foss waterfall, a beauty spot at Malham

inset (right): The River Aire on its course through Malham

Theakston's Wellgarth Brewery
MASHAM NORTH YORKSHIRE
circa 1830

Guesthouses: Bank Villa, tel. Ripon 89605
Self Catering: Abbey, Penhill and Witton Flats, tel. Bedale 60313
The Coach House, tel. Ripon 89327
Hedmark and Telemark, tel. Ripon 89335
Nelson House, Market Square, tel. Ripon 89327
Sunnyside Cottage, tel. Ripon 89327
Garages: Wensleydale (Todd and Sons), tel. Ripon 89202

Middleham

Map Ref: 87SE1287

Historically, and in the eyes of its 600 inhabitants, Middleham is a township, but with the friendly qualities of a village. Two miles south of Leyburn, on the A6108, it has grown up beneath the protection of its castle whose massive Norman keep dominates the grey stone houses and partially cobbled market squares. If mute stones had voice they would tell of medieval knights and their ladies, the proud Nevilles, the comings and goings of a royal prince, of fairs and festivals, romance and tragedy, trade and commerce, and the generations of townsfolk who had lived their days among the green fields of lower Wensleydale.

The first castle, its site marked by hawthorns, was built in early Norman times. Its successor of 1170 passed into the hands of the Nevilles of Raby a century later, but saw its great days during the Wars of the Roses. In 1461 the young Duke of Gloucester, later Richard III, joined the Middleham household for training and tutorage under the Earl of Warwick, subsequently courting and marrying his daughter Anne in 1472. They made their home at Middleham and their only son, Edward, was born here in 1473. They remained here until 1483; the year that Richard was crowned. He returned north only once more, on the death of his son in 1484. Anne died shortly afterwards, and Richard was slain at Bosworth in 1485. The castle remained Crown property until 1625, eventually passing into private hands, and is now in the guardianship of the Department of the Environment.

The Swine Cross in Middleham's upper market place commemorates Richard's 1479 ratification of the Market Charter given to the town a century earlier by Ralph Neville, Earl of Westmorland. A lane nearby leads to St Alkelda's Church, mainly 13th and 14th century, and made a collegiate foundation by Richard in 1478, continuing thus until the middle of last century, when Charles Kingsley was its last canon.

Three-storey Georgian houses and inns, particularly round the main Market Square, impart an urbane appearance to Middleham. Colourful window-surrounds brighten grey stone façades, and varied roof-lines add visual rhythm.

Masham

Map Ref: SE2280

Travellers entering the Yorkshire Dales from the south and east via Ripon and the A6108, cross the river Ure at Masham (pronounced Mass'm) but only skirt the town. Although some distance from the real beginnings of Wensleydale Masham has for centuries been an important market centre at the eastern edge of the Dales. In the century following the Conquest the de Mowbrays, based on Kirkby Malzeard, owned Mashamshire, but Masham's importance increased during medieval times through the influence of the nearby abbeys of Fountains and Jervaulx, each of which had many granges and estates in the district. Between 1250 and 1632 the town acquired a series of charters for markets and fairs, most of which were free from tolls, thus gaining trade at the expense of other local markets. By the 18th and 19th centuries Masham's great annual sheep fair in mid-September had grown to be one of the biggest in the north of England, with up to 70,000 sheep and lambs changing hands. They were brought on foot from Swaledale, Wensleydale and Nidderdale, using the old drove roads, most of which are now metalled.

Even into this century Masham's huge, square Market Place would be filled with sheep-pens during the September Fair, and every hotel, house and cottage with spare rooms would be filled. Gypsies camped by the river in what is now a popular open space for summer picnics; there were great family reunions; buyers came from far afield; the church bells were rung.

Theakston's Old Peculier has brought new fame to Masham, (top right), once known only for its market

The great Market Place, partly cobbled, remains Masham's outstanding feature. Surrounded by hotels, inns and houses of grey-brown stone it retains a degree of dignity. A small, tree-shaded market-cross is a focus, an island group of houses and shops a foil that breaks up the space. At a corner of the square St Mary's church looks south into open countryside. The lower part of its tower is Norman, with an octagonal 15th-century bell-stage added, together with a tall spire – an unusual feature in the Dales area. Outside the south door is the shaft of an important 9th-century Anglo-Saxon cross, showing four tiers of finely-carved figures, human and animal. A Gothick-style school of 1834 by the eastern exit from the square, and terraces of good stone cottages along the road to Kirkby Malzeard complete the impression of an attractive, spacious market-town. Masham is also the home of Theakston's, an independent family brewery since 1827, whose most potent brew, 'Old Peculier', has brought new distinction to the town, and in its name commemorates the fact that Masham was a 'peculier' from Roger de Mowbray's time, when the Archbishop of York freed it from 'all customs and claims of his archdeacon and officials.' It was thus allowed to have its own 'Peculier Court' – an ecclesiastical body with wide powers.

AA recommends:
Hotels: Jervaulx Hall, 2-star, Country House Hotel, tel. Bedale 60235

Racehorses in training on Middleham Low Moor

Most of the town is a Conservation Area, and behind the frontage narrow alleys hint at former concentrations of cottages.

Near the castle the farrier is kept busy for Middleham is one of the north's great centres for racehorse-training, a tradition going back two centuries. Many Georgian houses in and near the town are trainers' homes, and one set of stables adjoins the castle walls. Over 200 horses are currently trained at Middleham and can be expected at exercise during the mornings on local roads. To the west of the town the 363 acres of Middleham Low Moor provide splendid gallops, the courses marked by lines of whin bushes; High Moor, a few miles to the west, is used more during summer months. Low Moor was the site of one of the great

northern cattle fairs, held in late October and lasting three days, cattle sold on the first day, sheep on the second, and odds and ends on the third. It continued to attract large numbers of people until the end of last century but is now only a memory. The road over Middleham Low Moor leads to Coverdale.

AA recommends:
Hotels: Millers House, Market Place, 2-star, *tel.* Wensleydale 22630

Muker

Map Ref: 85SD9097

Largest of a trio of delightful villages near the head of Swaledale (the others are Thwaite and Keld),

Muker is situated at the southern foot of Kisdon, an isolated hill over 1600 feet high. The valley road from Reeth, B6270, continues westwards to Thwaite, then by the west side of Kisdon to Keld. The River Swale follows a beautiful valley course to the east of Kisdon and below Muker is joined by Muker Beck.

Grey stone cottages, a popular pub, a church built during Elizabeth's reign, a chapel and an Institute – village additions during lead-mining days last century – comprise Muker. Little there may be of architectural pretension but the group in its setting is memorable, with hills, valley and river in noble harmony.

Behind the village are some of the finest traditional hay-meadows in the Dales. In summer they show a rich variety of flowers and grasses, with up to a score of different species. To follow the footpath across them (single-file!) and squeeze through a series of narrow stone stiles, is one of the great summertime experiences in the Dales. To continue by the riverside to Keld, returning along the opposite side or by the Pennine Way track high on Kisdon's eastern shoulder, is the best walk in Swaledale. It is small wonder that this district inspired the Kearton brothers (Richard, 1862–1928 and Cherry, 1871–1940), who went to the village school in Muker, to devote their lives to watching wildlife, pioneering the photography of birds and animals, writing and lecturing about their experiences. They are commemorated by plaques on the chapel at Muker.

Wild Flowers

Vegetation imposes its own broad colour-scheme on the Dales landscape, and the type of vegetation is dictated by the soils and rocks beneath. Where there is gritstone, as above Nidderdale, Swaledale, and on the higher fells, there are sombre moors, dark for much of the year, purple with heather in August, and often associated with bracken along the edges. But in the limestone country of Craven, Malham and Wharfedale lightness and greenness set the scene, broken by ash woods on the scars. These contrasting colour masses touch on the science of ecology – the relationship of living things to their environment and to one another.

The relatively few plant species of the high fells – called mosses – are dominated by cotton-grass, with heather, bilberry and heath. True heather-moors occur between 1000 and 1400 feet, sometimes reaching to 1700, and down to 700 feet on the descending eastern ridges, where tormentil, eyebrights, trefoils and vetches add splashes of colour to grassy swards at the heather's edge.

No one species dominates the limestone, and there is more variety, more colour. Where limestone

pastures are heavily grazed by sheep, the turf stays short and many small-stemmed plants flourish. In rough, un-grazed grassland plants that can compete with the taller grasses may be seen; unmown roadside verges and hay-meadows before cutting provide similar habitats, favoured by knapweed, harebells, early purple orchid, sneezewort and occasionally cowslip. Limestone country is not densely wooded, but the ash which dominates the scars casts only a light shade so that plants which like the damp, lime-rich soils of this woodland floor flourish in such conditions – ramsons, lily-of-the-valley, yellow pimpernel and giant bell-flower. The same ashwoods are also rich in shrub species.

In more acid areas where the parent rock is sandstone or slate foxgloves can be expected on banksides and in

Lime-rich soils feed (left to right) yellow pimpernel, giant bell-flower, ramsons, and ash.

open clearings. Sessile oaks are the dominant trees, and beneath their heavier leaf canopy fewer ground species grow. Wensleydale, and to some extent Swaledale, with their Yoredale strata of rocks, provide a greater variety of habitat than the other dales, but wherever wild flowers are seen it needs to be remembered that it is now illegal to uproot any wild plant, and even the picking of rare species is prohibited by law. If a flower is picked the seeds from which next season's plants would grow will not be formed. In any case, wild flowers look their best in their natural surroundings.

Birds of the Dales

The variety of bird life in the Dales reflects the range of landscape habitats. Along most rivers and their tributaries pied and grey wagtails, dippers and common sandpipers can be seen; oyster-catchers nest on shingle banks in the upper reaches and the occasional heron is more likely to be spotted in flight than as a silent, grey sentinel, fish-watching.

Top: Dippers live on upland streams
Bottom: A curlew tending its young

Stone walls are no substitute for the good cover that hedgerows normally provide, although wheatears do like them as perches and song-posts. Deciduous woodlands in gills, on scars, as copses or shelter-belts offer suitable cover for blackbirds, thrushes, redstarts, chaffinches, willow-warblers, spotted and pied fly-catchers, nuthatches, tree-creepers, various tits as well as for the larger birds – rooks, jackdaws, wood-pigeons, green and spotted wood-peckers, though these latter are more likely to be heard than seen. One of the smallest birds, the meadow-pipit, probably has the widest habitat range, and skylarks are also widespread.

Swifts, swallows and house-martins add grace to summer skies, but it is the haunting calls of curlew, lapwing, golden plover and redshank which evoke most vividly the lonelier uplands, the high fells and mosses. Heather moors echo to the harsh rasp of grouse, and it is the elegant black-headed gull which has taken over as breeding-grounds the sky-reflecting tarns of the uplands, coming down to valley fields to feed.

Of birds of prey kestrels are probably the commonest at lower levels, sparrow-hawks less so, while in the remote places buzzards seem to be more numerous than ravens. Most of the predators are holding their own but you need to be sharp to spot merlins, peregrines or short-eared owls.

Nidderdale

Map Ref: SE0676 to SE2459

When the Yorkshire Dales National Park was designated in 1954 its eastern boundary was drawn to exclude Nidderdale, presumably because most of the valley above Pateley Bridge, and the surrounding watershed of the Nidd, are associated with providing water for the City of Bradford, and as a result public access to the hills is limited. Nevertheless, the reservoirs – Gouthwaite (1901), Scar House (1936) and Angram (1919) – impart to Nidderdale, even if artificially, a new element to the landscape which differentiates it from the other dales.

Before they entered the scene Nidderdale was the most industrialised of the major Yorkshire dales based on flax-growing and the manufacture of linen and hemp. In addition lead-ore was mined and smelted among the hills to the west, but in the upper dale farming predominated, as it still does. The minor road to the upper dale from Pateley Bridge keeps to the western side of the river, passes Foster Beck Mill, now an inn, but retaining its huge over-shot waterwheel, and winds by the side of Gouthwaite Reservoir. This enlargement of a natural lake is a favourite place for wading birds and waterfowl, especially during the winter months, where they like the expanses of mud and marsh at the shallow northern end. Roadside parking is very restricted; a walk from Wath to Bouthwaite along the eastern side of the lake (three miles) is a more rewarding way of seeing the wildlife.

At the head of the lake Ramsgill is Nidderdale's prettiest village, with grey-stone houses informally grouped round two greens separated by a small beck. Daffodils dazzle in late April, and trees provide summer shade. Tall, Tudor-style chimneys on the Yorke Arms are unusual accents in a charming village-scape. Two miles beyond, Lofthouse and Middlesmoor are the end villages of the dale, the former's stone cottages and farms huddle at the foot of the steep hill which takes an open moorland road over to Masham in Wensleydale. Middlesmoor's distinction is that it can be reached only by a one-in-four gradient to its hillside perch. Anglican church, Wesleyan chapel, and close-clustered cottages occupy one of the most exposed, windswept village sites in the Dales, 1000 feet above sea-level. The road ends here. However, from Lofthouse a toll road (ticket machine) allows motorists to drive four miles up the valley to Scar House Reservoir, where there are car-parking facilities, picnic areas, and the possible pleasure of a walk round the edge of the reservoir, crossing above it by Angram dam.

Because of the remote situation of these two upland reservoirs a railway was essential to carry building materials during their construction. The Nidd Valley Light Railway was opened in 1907 with a public section between Pateley Bridge and Lofthouse, and a private, waterworks section to the reservoir sites. This had to negotiate 1 in 40 gradients. With Bradford Corporation owning it, the Nidd Valley Line was the only British example of a municipality operating a passenger-carrying railway. After the reservoirs were completed the track was kept open for villagers and tourists, finally closing in 1936, and its course can still be identified.

Near Lofthouse is the spectacular How Stean Gorge, recently developed as a visitor centre. How Stean Beck runs between 70-feet rocky cliffs; footpaths, bridges on different levels, and fenced galleries on rocky ledges allow the chasm to be explored. There is a children's play area nearby.

Pateley Bridge

Map Ref: 97SE1565

Good roads converge on this small town of dour buildings of local gritstone. The B6165 from Harrogate and B6451 from Otley, meeting at Summer Bridge, are joined near Pateley by the B6265 from Ripon, which continues westwards over Greenhow Hill to Grassington. In medieval times monastic estates nearby helped to promote good communications, and Pateley's sheltered situation on the north bank of the Nidd, on the frontier between upland and lowland farming, merited its development as a market centre from the 14th century. Heights of its industrial prosperity were reached about 1800, but when the textile industry became mechanised, its water-powered mills could not compete with steam-

Pateley Bridge is served by good roads

powered ones nearer the coalfields. Linen manufacture decreased and Pateley's mills turned to making cord, twine and rope. Stone quarrying and mineral working – mainly lead – survived through last century, but Pateley's present prosperity is based largely on agriculture and tourism. Its fortnightly livestock market survives, and on the Monday nearest to 20 September is Nidderdale Agricultural Society's Annual Show.

Pateley's only medieval building, the old church of St Mary, high above the town, is in roofless decay, abandoned in 1827 when the present church was built in the town. The Panorama Walk nearby commands extensive views of Nidderdale and the moors around, and for those who prefer the riverside there is a convenient free car park at the bottom of the main street. The Nidderdale Museum, recently established, houses a good collection of folk exhibits displayed in seven large rooms, illustrating all aspects of Nidderdale life in the past. Nearby, the Primitive Methodist Chapel has been converted into the Pateley Bridge Dramatic Society's own theatre. Across the river in Bewerley is the early 16th-century chapel which belonged to Fountains Abbey.

AA recommends:
Self Catering: Curlew, Robins Rest and Throstle Nest Cottages, Highfold, Glasshouses, tel. Harrogate 711328
Guesthouses: Grassfields Country House Hotel, tel. Harrogate 711412

Redmire

Map Ref: 86SE0491

Five miles west of Leyburn the minor road along the northern side of Wensleydale makes sharp bends through Redmire, whose main axis, unusually, lies north-south. One outcome of this is that a number of houses down its eastern side are built gable-end to the road, allowing them to face southwards across the valley to the broad, flat-topped bulk of Penhill. Footpaths cross a small, tree-shaded green where the stepped plinth of a vanished cross now supports a Victorian jubilee pillar of 1887, crowned with the recent addition of a lamp.

Narrow lanes bordered by unpretentious cottages of grey stone lead out of the village beyond the green. One of them passes the smithy and the Bolton Arms, leading to Castle Bolton and the moorland road to Grinton in Swaledale. The other passes the King's Arms and the Post Office, which was originally built in 1862 as a drill-hall for Volunteers. In the 18th and 19th centuries Redmire was largely an industrial village of craftsmen, lead-miners and coal-miners who worked at the mines and pits whose remains scar the moors to the north. Today, flower and vegetable gardens give Redmire a degree of colour which makes it less austere than most Wensleydale villages.

Half a mile away to the south-east is the parish church of St Michael, remote and rural, a simple building with a good Norman doorway.

Reeth

Map Ref: 80SE0399

A dozen miles west of Richmond, by one of the most scenic valley roads in the Dales, Swaledale divides, with Arkengarthdale branching to the north-west and the main valley continuing due west to Muker and Keld. Reeth occupies a commanding position on the lower slopes of Calva, uniting the two valleys but with its feet almost in the Arkle Beck. This

Reeth, once thriving, is now known for its open views. From here a suspension footbridge swings over the River Swale

gateway situation led to the granting of a market charter in 1695, and in the two centuries which followed it became an important centre of farming and industry, when hand-knitting and lead-mining thrived. The village expanded, and seven fairs and a Friday market were held. Now, the population has fallen from 1300 to 350; Reeth Show in September and the autumn sheep sales are the main annual events, but summer weekends see Reeth Green thronged with people who come just to enjoy the superb setting.

Three-storey houses and inns along High Row testify to Reeth's 18th-century growth which was helped by the turnpiking in 1741 of the Arkengarthdale road from Tan Hill. Houses fringe the sloping green, at whose lower end a former Methodist Schoolroom houses the Swaledale Folk Museum, whose range of exhibits illuminate many facets of the local history of Reeth and its neighbourhood. Paintings, pottery and local crafts are exhibited for sale in three local shops or galleries, while beyond the village field and riverside paths are an enticement to walkers.

AA recommends:
Hotels: Punch Bowl, 1-star, tel. Richmond 86233 (4 miles W on B6270 at Low Row)

Ribblesdale

Map Ref: SD7678 to SD8163

Yorkshire's famous Three Peaks, Ingleborough, Whernside and Pen-y-ghent, look loftily if distantly down on Ribble Head, where the road down Ribblesdale, B6479, branches off the Hawes-Ingleton road, B6255, near the great railway viaduct. The river is born near Ribble Head House and follows a winding course southwards to Settle, its valley given character by Ingleton to the west and Pen-y-ghent on the east. Low outcropping scars of limestone glisten in sunlight; to the east a huge area of hummocky land extending down the valley almost to Horton, with low, rounded hills 50–150 feet high, represents the boulder-filled drumlins left by a retreating glacier. It was difficult land to farm so there are no settlements in the upper valley, only scattered farms, this dispersal extending northwards beyond Ribble Head to the feet of Whernside.

Selside is the first hamlet in the dale, where the narrow road twists between two or three farms, and the railway line is close. Other farms nearby underline the fact that this is almost wholly a farming community, and has been since Norse settlers came here a thousand years ago. The railway is only the most recent (1876) of a succession of routes up

Richmond (below) has many military links, despite knowing neither siege nor attack. Right: Green Howards uniform

Ribblesdale – Roman, monastic, medieval, packhorse, drove and turnpike. Many of the old tracks are now green lanes, to Wharfedale, Wensleydale and Crummackdale.

Horton is Ribblesdale's chief village. Below it the valley narrows, the scars of quarrying gash the hillsides above Horton and Helwith Bridge, from where narrow lanes lead westwards to Austwick, and the valley's western side to Settle. Slate was quarried at Helwith Bridge and used as cottage floors, doorsteps, porches, gateposts, roofs and headstones, and can be identified in many buildings of Ribblesdale. The main road continues down the east side of the valley touching Stainforth and Langcliffe (see separate entries) before reaching Settle.

The graceful arches of the Ribblehead viaduct can be seen for miles around

Richmond

Map Ref: 81NZ1701

High above the River Swale Richmond's hill-top situation gives it a visual excitement rarely matched in England. Its stones and street-pattern enshrine nine busy centuries of history, imparting a unique character, and making it pre-eminent as a gateway to the Dales. Richmond is more than a lively market town: it is an experience. From the A1 at Scotch Corner the A6108 reaches Richmond in four miles, entering the town from the north-east. Only the southern approach, by A6136 from Catterick, provides the dramatic view of the castle on the rock, and it is the castle (Department of Environment) which commands the scene.

From every angle Richmond's Norman castle dominates the town. At its south-east corner Scolland's Hall, late 11th century, is probably the oldest hall in England. The massive keep, built a century later, and unusual in being at the gatehouse, gives the finest prospect of Richmond from its 100-feet high battlements. Far below are the roofs, walls and chimneys, a pattern of pink pantiles, stone slates and Welsh slates. The well-defined limits of the Market Place follow the line of walls of the castle's outer bailey. The medieval town walls were about fifty yards beyond them, but only fragments survive, including gateways on Cornforth Hill and in Friar's Wynd.

Narrow streets radiate from the Market Place. New Road, which was new in the 18th century to provide better access to Green Bridge; Finkle Street, one of the medieval streets leading to Newbiggin, new in the 12th century and now Richmond's most elegant thoroughfare, with trees and good Georgian houses; King Street, which dates from 1813, and Frenchgate, the oldest way into the town, but today lined with elegant houses which illustrate the town's commercial and social development during the 18th century. Details in doorways and windows delight the eye, and everything is in small-town scale – except of course, the castle, the splendid view from Castle Walk, and the distant Swaledale scenery to the west, along the wooded valley and past Culloden Tower's distinctive shape.

Unusually, St Mary's parish church lay outside the town walls. Holy Trinity, islanded in the Market Place, was never more than a chapel, and now houses the Green Howards Museum. Apart from it and the castle Richmond's only other medieval building is Grey Friars' Tower, all that remains of a Franciscan Friary. Opposite this is a rare treasure, the Georgian Theatre, dating from 1788 and restored to theatrical use in 1963. Regular productions are presented on its tiny stage before audiences of up to 240 who occupy many of the original seats and boxes in one of the oldest surviving theatre buildings in the country. Although the Market Place provides limited car-parking, long-stay visitors are advised to use the large free car park along Victoria Road, 400 yards west of the King Street roundabout.

AA recommends:
Hotels: Frenchgate, 59–61 Frenchgate, 2-star, *tel.* Richmond 2087
King's Head, Market Square, 2-star, *tel.* Richmond 2311
Campsites: Swale View Caravan Site, Reeth Road, 2-pennants, *tel.* Richmond 3106
Garages: Victoria Road Garage, Victoria Road, *tel.* Richmond 2539

Sedbergh

Map Ref: 82SD6592

Five miles east of M6 (Junction 37) Sedbergh is the main western gateway to the Dales, and lies just within the National Park boundary. Its position on the A684 Kendal–Northallerton road which cleaves through Garsdale and Wensleydale has further increased its tourist

potential as a good base from which to explore the western areas of the Yorkshire Dales, a fact recognised by its good range of accommodation – hotels, guesthouses, holiday cottages, caravan and campsites. Sheltered to the north by the steep-sided Howgills, Sedbergh is the only settlement in the Rawthey valley. The river flows down the eastern side of the hills, partnered by the A683 from Kirkby Stephen, is joined near the town by the Clough River from Garsdale, and Dentdale's River Dee, the combined waters amalgamating with those of the Lune two miles to the south-west.

Above Sedbergh's north-eastern corner Castlehaw was the site of a Norman motte-and-bailey castle. In the town centre, the parish church has Norman origins, and the miniscule Market Place claims charter rights dating from 1251. The main area of weekly stalls (Wednesdays) is in the Joss Lane car park (free) at the eastern end of town. A large livestock market operates from premises in the Kendal road. There is another large car park (free) by the Dent road.

Farms are widely scattered in the valley country around Sedbergh. During the 17th, 18th, and early 19th centuries they formed part of the domestic knitting trade which flourished locally. To this was added a cotton industry, based on mills built at Birks, Millthrop, and Howgill. A woollen mill was built at Hebblethwaite Hall, and in Sedbergh itself houses were crammed into yards behind the main street. Upper storeys had wooden balconies called spinning-galleries, while lower floors were let as stables, stores and workshops. At least one spinning-gallery survives.

In 1525, a famous date for Sedbergh, Roger Lupton, a native of the parish and provost of Eton, founded a chantry school, endowing it with scholarships and fellowships at St John's College, Cambridge. It

The Friends' Meeting House at Brigflatts has an aura of humble devotion

became a free grammar-school in 1552, was rebuilt in 1716, and re-constituted as a Public School in 1874, since when it has gained a national reputation. School buildings and playing fields cover most of Sedbergh's southern fringe, but public rights-of-way through the fields are maintained. The original 1716 building on the Dent road is now a library and museum.

Sedbergh has strong Quaker associations, and George Fox preached in the district on many occasions, the most famous one being at Firbank in 1652. Two miles from Sedbergh is Brigflatts, formerly a small industrial community, and its exquisite Friends' Meeting House of 1675, the oldest in the north of England, retains many original furnishings, in an atmosphere of calm, cool tranquillity.

AA recommends:
Campsites: Pinfold Caravan Park, 3-pennants, *tel.* Sedbergh 20576
Self Catering: The Hylands, *tel.* Hull 493875
13 Queens Drive, *tel.* Hertford 465185
Garages: Sedbergh Motor Company, Station Road, *tel.* Sedbergh 20678 (day) and 20322 (night)

National Park Centres

Six National Park Centres have been created to provide visitors with information about the Yorkshire Dales in general, with each Centre having detailed information about its own location in particular. At the Centres at Aysgarth, Hawes, Grassington, Malham and Clapham large car parks are available on a fee-paying basis. The car park ticket allows use at all National Park car parks on the day of issue. The Sedbergh Centre adjoins a large free public car park entered from Joss Lane.

Centres are open daily from Easter to September, each is staffed by an Information Assistant, and each usually houses an interpretative display relating to its specific area. The Malham Centre was purpose-built in 1975 and offers an audio-visual display, particularly useful for visiting school parties. Other centres occupy

buildings converted from other use – railway buildings at Aysgarth and Hawes, the old manor-house at Clapham, a cottage at Sedbergh, while at Grassington it is housed in an annexe to the National Park office.

From various Centres throughout the season, with concentrations at Bank Holidays and during July and August, a programme of Guided Walks is arranged. These start at 2pm and usually last 2½–3 hours. Guides are local people with special interest in some aspect of the Dales – local history, flowers, birds, farming, buildings, old industries. The cost is minimal, and pre-booking is not necessary. Groups are usually limited to about twenty, and dogs are dis-couraged! Information about Guided Walks is given in a free publication *The Visitor*.

The Yorkshire Dales National Park's emblem is a Swaledale ram

Yorkshire Dales National Park

Semer Water is a large glacial lake

Semer Water

Map Ref: 85SD9187

A honeypot for summer crowds, a sanctuary for winter wildfowl, Semer Water is the largest natural lake in Yorkshire, half a mile long, and on the south side of Wensleydale. Twin roads from Bainbridge lead to the lake, following opposite sides of England's shortest river, the Bain. A link between them touches Semer Water's northern shore, its only access point. Cars can park (charge), and the lake attracts canoers, wind-surfers, yachtsmen and fishermen. Children paddle safely, and swimmers brave the cool, shallow

waters in summer.

Countersett, on the western road to Semer Water, has strong Quaker associations, with a Friends' Meeting House and some good 17th-century houses, including the Hall, 1650, with its two-storeyed porch and stone-mullioned windows. This road ends at Marsett, at the foot of beautiful little Bardale. Above Semer Water's eastern side the road ends at Stalling Busk – merely 'Busk' to locals (it means 'bush') – a hill-clinging community of farms and cottages, with an unusual ruined church in the fields below, and a Roman road climbing the Stake pass above, to Buckden in Wharfedale. The broad, flat valley above the head of Semer Water is Raydale, enclosed by high, lonely fells whose lower sides are now darkened with conifer plantations.

Settle

Map Ref: 94SD8163

Like other market-towns in the Dales Settle developed and prospered through its situation between the livestock farming of the uplands and the mixed and arable farming of the lower parts of its valley, in this case the Ribble. Today it benefits – or suffers, depending on your point of view – from being on

the A65 Keighley-Kendal road – busy not only with freight traffic but also with the increasing volume of holiday traffic to and from the Lake District as well as the cars of visitors entering the Dales from the south.

Settle's market charter goes back to 1249, granted for it to serve Ribblesdale and Craven. Market day is Tuesday, when the Market Square is filled with colourful stalls, looked down upon by the unusual, two-storey Shambles, whose arches are probably mid-18th century but whose cottages were raised by a storey late last century. Many stalls and shops support local crafts; expect to find needlework, tapestry, pottery, hand-made jewellery, lampshades and fleeces. Almost all Settle shops are small, independent, with many having been in the same family for generations.

Two factors contribute to Settle's 'family atmosphere'. It has remained small, compact and intimate, and it has been faithful to its past, not having destroyed those buildings from the late 17th century onwards which are so important a part of its character. A large free car park on the town's southern edge is not the least of Settle's advantages.

Following the short streets leading from the Market Place – Constitution Hill and Castle Hill, High Street, Victoria Street and Albert Street, which were the old ways into town; Chapel Street, Station Road and Kirkgate – will reveal the yards and squares, cottages, small houses and

Dales Rail
The Settle–Carlisle Line

Railway historians suggest that the Settle–Carlisle line should never have been built. It arose from a quarrel between two companies, the Midland, and the London & North-Western, but built it was, by the Midland, between 1869 and 1876. Constructionally the most difficult, scenically the most dramatic in England, the line follows the Ribble valley above Settle – the famous 'long drag' to Ribble Head, across the heads of Dentdale, Garsdale and Wensleydale, and down Mallerstang to the Vale of Eden and Carlisle. At Garsdale Head it reaches 1100 feet, yet the ruling gradient never exceeds 1 in 100. Towering viaducts and bridges, and long, deep tunnels represent an heroic example of Victorian engineering, busy with freight and passenger trains for almost a century.

The 1963 Beeching Report started

the decline in its use, and local services ceased by 1970 leaving only Settle and Appleby stations open to be served by through trains. However, limited passenger services were revived a few years later, through the combined efforts of the Yorkshire Dales National Park Committee, the West Yorkshire Passenger Transport Executive, the Countryside Commission, and the County Councils of Lancashire and Cumbria. Dales Rail was born and for ten years has increasingly thrived. On the first weekend of every month from April to October diesel railcars from towns in West Yorkshire and Lancashire carry visitors to the Dales. Trains stop at Settle and Appleby, and some specially opened intermediate stations. Eden valley stations to Carlisle are used on Saturdays only, while also on Saturdays only a bus service links with trains from Garsdale Station to Sedbergh and to Leyburn,

and on Sundays only a bus service operates between Garsdale Station and Richmond, via Hawes and Wensleydale. On some days extra bus services provide a link with Teesdale, Tynedale and the Northern Pennines. Some National Park Guided Walks are planned to start and finish from stations along the line.

Thus, Dales Rail meets the needs of town-dwellers wishing to travel to the Dales and walk in the area, without their having to use their own transport. Each train's immediate return to its place of origin allows Dales residents the chance to have a day in town or city.

The Glasgow St Enoch to St Pancras express on the Settle-Carlisle line in 1911

workshops which represent the rapid growth in activity from 1780 onwards, when the development of local crafts, trades and industries reduced Settle's reliance on farming.

By far the most outstanding building is The Folly of 1675, a capricious extravaganza of windows and fine masonry, Tudor in appearance, quite out of Dales character, but undeniably fascinating. It now houses an antiques showroom. A Georgian warehouse overlooks Cheapside, and other Georgian buildings testify to Settle's growing importance when the Keighley-Kendal Turnpike brought the coaching traffic to the town, and the resultant need for hotels and inns with which Settle is still blessed. Observant explorers will notice the happy survival of many dated 17th-century door-heads, while the really energetic may accept the challenge of a short steep climb to the wooded top of Castleberg, a limestone crag above the town, with rewarding panoramic views.

Skipton Castle's round-towered gateway is surmounted by the Clifford motto 'Desormais' meaning 'henceforth'

AA recommends:
Hotels: Falcon Manor, Skipton Road, 3-star, *tel.* Settle 3814
Royal Oak, Market Place, 2-star, *tel.* Settle 2561
Garages: West Yorkshire (F H Ellis), *tel.* Settle 2529 (day) and 2585 (night)

Skipton

Map Ref: 96SD9851

With the rich limestone pastures of the Craven uplands to the north, gritstone moors to the south, the broad pastoral lowlands of the Ribble vale a dozen miles to the west, Skipton's situation in the Aire gap ensured its importance as a frontier town, with all the advantages arising from this. Today, major trunk roads meet and cross at Skipton: A59 Preston-Harrogate, A65 Leeds-Kendal, A56 from Burnley, A629 from Keighley. With the B6265 heading north to Grassington, Skipton rightly regards itself as the southern gateway to the Dales, only two miles outside the National Park boundary. A new by-pass has eliminated much through traffic from the town, whose main general market is on Saturday, with stalls in the High Street also operating on Monday, Wednesday and Friday.

A village settled by Anglian sheep-farmers in the 7th century it became, in the 12th century, a Norman castle-town under the de Romilles who built their fortress on a rock above the Eller Beck gorge. A market was established at the top of what is now High Street, and a three-day annual fair soon followed. Weekly markets concentrated on perishable goods, fairs were more seasonal, dealing with bigger quantities of different commodities – wool, fabrics, metals, leather, salt, wine – bringing traders and merchants from further afield than those involved in the weekly market which was a more local affair. From the 13th to the 18th centuries a town like Skipton with good markets and fairs was virtually self-supporting.

The parish church grew up contiguous with the castle, and the town developed down High Street. In 1309 the castle passed into the hands of the Cliffords, and remained their main home for three and a half centuries. It is still in private hands, open daily, and visitors receive a 40-sketch tour sheet to indicate the most practical viewing route. A very informative descriptive booklet is also available. Entrance is by the proud round-towered gateway surmounted by the Clifford motto, 'Desormais', meaning, roughly, 'henceforth'. After the Civil War Lady Anne Clifford rebuilt the partially-ruined castle, and much of what can be viewed dates from 1655–58, and is splendidly-restored.

Many High Street properties were rebuilt in the second half of the 17th century, and in the 1720s weavers and wool-combers built houses at the bottom end of the town. Thirty years later the Keighley-Kendal Turnpike increased Skipton's importance as a wool trading centre, with a livestock market, and by the end of the century the Leeds-Liverpool Canal ensured the concentration of the worsted cloth industry in the town. In 1785, High Mill near the castle was opened as a cotton-spinning mill and early in the 19th century new mills were built by the canal banks. The associated labour needs brought a rapid population growth, long gardens behind High Street properties were in-filled, and many of their yards survive, especially on the west side, tunnel-like openings leading to narrow alleyways with terraced houses along them. Large cotton-mills were added to Skipton's townscape between 1850–80, with terrace developments of gritstone houses on the south-eastern slopes above the canal. The town's population doubled from 6000 in 1871 to 13,000 in 1911, and has stabilised at this figure.

Good parking facilities encourage a long stay and an exploration of the town, appreciating its friendliness, its human scale and lively market-stalls.

AA recommends:
Hotels: Midland, Broughton Road, 1-star, *tel.* Skipton 2781
Anchor Inn, 2-star, *tel.* Gargrave 666 (4 miles NW on A65 at Gargrave)
Restaurants: Le Caveau, 86 High Street, 1-fork, *tel.* Skipton 4274
Campsites: Overdale Trailer Park, 3-pennants, Harrogate Road, *tel.* Skipton 3480
Guesthouses: Craven House, 56 Keighley Road, *tel.* Skipton 4657
Fairleigh, 24 Belle Vue Terrace, Broughton Road, *tel.* Skipton 4153
Highfield Hotel, 58 Keighley Road, *tel.* Skipton 3182
Unicorn Hotel, Keighley Road, *tel.* Skipton 4146
Red Lion Hotel (Inn), High Street, *tel.* Skipton 60718
Kirk Skye, 19 High Street, *tel.* Gargrave 356 (4 miles SW on A65 at Gargrave)
Garages: Carleton, Otley Road, *tel.* Skipton 2807 (day) and 61340 (night)
P Clarke Autos, Carleton New Road, *tel.* Skipton 5531 (day) and 60228 (night)
Forge, Bolton Bridge, *tel.* Bolton Abbey 221 (day) and Barnoldswick 813956 (night)
Skipton Service Station (E S Hartley), Keighley Road, *tel.* Skipton 2162

The packhorse bridge connecting Great Stainforth and Little Stainforth

branch to Malham, while on the west side of Ribblesdale narrow lanes from Little Stainforth lead to Helwith Bridge and Austwick, as well as to Settle.

AA recommends:
Campsites: Knight Stainforth Hall Caravan and Camp Site, 3-pennants, *tel.* Settle 2200

Stainforth

Map Ref: 94SD8267

Its name derives from the 'stony ford' which linked two settlements half a mile apart on opposite banks of the Ribble north of Settle. Stainforth, on the eastern side, was formerly owned by Sawley Abbey, whose monks developed the estate which prospered, while Little Stainforth, under private ownership, declined. In the 1670s, Samuel Watson replaced the ford by a packhorse bridge whose graceful arch (National Trust) spans an attractively wooded stretch of the river, and a grassy path

leads downstream to Stainforth Force, where the river falls over limestone ledges into a deep, broad pool. In Little Stainforth the rather forbidding, three-storey Stainforth Hall was built at the same time and is now occupied as a farmhouse.

Stainforth village is by-passed by the B6479, but a large free car park is an encouragement to stay and saunter among the grey stone cottages centred on a rough green by Cowside Beck, which is spanned by a little clapper bridge. Goat Scar Lane is a stony track leading to Catrigg Force on Stainforth Beck (1 mile); Goat Lane is a fine moorland road to Halton Gill in Littondale, with a

Swaledale

Map Ref: NY9000 to SE1199

Narrow, sinuous and austerely beautiful, Swaledale is the most northerly of Yorkshire's major dales. Richmond is its eastern gateway, 30 miles from the source of the Swale among the peat haggs and heather 2000 feet up on the lonely uplands of Birkdale Common. A journey westwards up the dale reveals how it is enfolded by unbroken ranges of hills, emphasising both its completeness and, towards the valley-head, its remoteness. Such a journey also shows the extent to which man has contributed to the landscape, from the hanging woods in the lower dale between Richmond and Reeth to the soaring stone walls, field barns, farms, villages and

Lead Mining

Veins of **lead ore** (galena = lead sulphide) exist in the limestone of the Lower Carboniferous Series, mainly between altitudes of 1000 and 2000 feet, but because they occur beneath the surface they had to be mined. The Romans worked them, monasteries held mining rights in medieval times, but the main period of activity was during the 18th and 19th centuries, peaking between 1790 and 1860. Most survivals date from then.

Ore-fields are concentrated in two areas; in the north Arkengarthdale, Swaledale and the north side of Wensleydale; in the south it extends from Buckden in Wharfedale eastwards to Pateley Bridge in Nidderdale. Early workings were from the surface by shallow bell-pits, later ones by horizontal adits driven into hillsides along the veins of ore. Suspected veins were revealed (or not) by hushing, a process of scouring a hillside with

water released from a temporary small reservoir impounded on the hilltop above. Repeated hushings have left huge gashes on hillsides, especially in Gunnerside Gill and above Langthwaite.

The mined mixture of ore and rock (called bouse) had to be crushed and

Main picture: Old Gang Smelt Mill
Inset: Lead ore crusher, Craven Museum

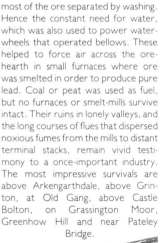

most of the ore separated by washing. Hence the constant need for water, which was also used to power waterwheels that operated bellows. These helped to force air across the orehearth in small furnaces where ore was smelted in order to produce pure lead. Coal or peat was used as fuel, but no furnaces or smelt-mills survive intact. Their ruins in lonely valleys, and the long courses of flues that dispersed noxious fumes from the mills to distant terminal stacks, remain vivid testimony to a once-important industry. The most impressive survivals are above Arkengarthdale, above Grinton, at Old Gang, above Castle Bolton, on Grassington Moor, Greenhow Hill and near Pateley Bridge.

remains of lead-mining which are so prominent in the upper dale.

The A6108, and then B6270, follow the winding river to Reeth, but the old road along the hills to the north, through Marske and Marrick, though more tortuous in places, is a more exciting way to Reeth. Here the valley divides, Arkengarthdale branching to the north-west and Swaledale aligned due west. A round trip up one and down the other is an excellent way of exploring this wild, northern section of the National Park, whose Pennine character becomes increasingly evident as the dale heads are approached.

Beyond Reeth the B6270 keeps to the northern side of Swaledale, through Healaugh, Feetham and Low Row to Gunnerside, where the road crosses to the south, continuing westwards to Muker. Then it leaves the river for a while to take a course through Thwaite and behind Kisdon, rejoining the Swale at Keld, the last village in the dale.
Placenames have their own music, a euphony originating from Norse settlement a thousand years ago. Every village, hamlet, farm and barn is of local grey-brown sandstone from small quarries hidden in the hills. Low-pitched roofs of stone flags echo distant skylines. Buildings are not beautiful, but their sturdy shapes and textures are in complete harmony with the surroundings.

Hay ripens in riverside meadows, cut in July and stored in a hundred barns. Farming and tourism are Swaledale's main industries now that centuries of lead-mining have ended. Field-paths and miners' tracks are invitations to explore Swaledale's intimate delights, particularly in the upper dale.

Above Keld the lonely road to the gathering-grounds of the infant river reveals a different world of bare, sweeping moors, sombre skylines and splendid solitude. It is wilderness country, a similar landscape to that experienced on the West Stonesdale road from Keld to Tan Hill where Britain's highest inn

has no neighbour for about four miles. Follow the road eastwards from here and it is five miles before the first enclosed fields appear, and Arkengarthdale's green valley shows its patterned hillsides. At Langthwaite scars and spoilheaps speak of vanished days of lead-mining, and the moorland road to Reeth threads its way between sheep-cropped verges. From the sturdy, black-faced Swaledale sheep comes the warm durable wool which has helped to revive a traditional hand-knitting industry developed over the past few years and boosted by tourism. Small hotels, village pubs, guesthouses, farms and holiday cottages provide a variety of accommodation for visitors who appreciate the serenity of this hauntingly-lovely valley, its sparkling river and becks, and the lonely, sheep-voiced hills.

Threshfield

Map Ref: 96SD9863

Across the river from Grassington, where the Wharfedale road through Burnsall, B6160, meets the busier road from Skipton, B6265, is Threshfield. The heart of the village is the Park, a small triangular remnant of green, with trees and stocks. Seventeenth-century houses and barns cluster round, especially on the eastern side. Date-panels signify much activity between 1640 and 1661, with Park Grange and the Manor House whose tall gable includes a lovely porch with Tudor-style rose window above, prominent. Nearby is a three-doorway barn, or shippon, dated 1661, while opposite is Old Hall Inn, 19th-century at the front, Georgian at the back. Behind it is the original Old Hall, now a store, possibly of 14th-century date. Threshfield Free Grammar School, founded in 1674 by the Reverend Matthew Hewitt, one of the two rectors of Linton, is by the back road

Swaledale's patterned hillsides are rich, green and hauntingly lovely

from Linton to Grassington that passes half a mile east of Threshfield, and a path leads to it from the village. This delightful little building is still in use as the primary school. Near the hump-backed bridge on the Skipton road a barn door is adorned with horse-shoes and cow-shoes of various sizes, a reminder of the packhorse and droving importance of Threshfield in past centuries.

Bordley Stone Circle, Threshfield

West of the village a narrow road, metalled for only three miles, leads past the hamlet of Skythorns and its associated limestone quarry, to Malham Moor. It continues as a green lane to join Mastiles Lane, important from medieval times to droving days last century. The remains of Bordley's prehistoric stone circle are near the end of the metalled road, but to reach the hamlet of Bordley, almost a mile away, footpaths or green lanes must be followed, for there is no road to this loneliest of hamlets on the Craven uplands.

AA recommends:
Hotels: Wilson Arms, 3-star, *tel.* Grassington 752666
Campsites: Long Ashes Caravan Park, 3-pennants, *tel.* Grassington 752261
Woodnook Caravan Park, Skythorns, *tel.* Skipton 752412
Self Catering: Glen Cottage, *tel.* Skipton 752412

A lintel commemorating pioneer wildlife photographers Richard and Cherry Kearton decorates the house where they were born in Thwaite (above)

Thwaite

Map Ref: 85SD8998

The road up Swaledale, B6270, takes a northward turn here, where clustered cottages by Thwaite Beck at the foot of Kisdon hill exemplify the characteristic rugged charm of a remote Dales village. A couple of farms, former lead-miners' homes that are now holiday cottages, and the well-known Kearton Guest House, comprise this friendly community. The Kearton brothers (see Muker entry) were born here, and a modern, delightfully-decorated lintel over a cottage doorway commemorates their birthplace.

Beyond the village the Pennine Way, having descended from Great Shunner Fell, climbs across the face of Kisdon to follow its exciting route above the Swale to Keld. The road takes an equally scenic course through a green landscape, patterned by walls and barns, past Angram to Keld. To the south the Butter Tubs Pass rises to 1725 feet on its wild, moorland crossing to Hawes in Wensleydale. Near the top of the pass, above a steep-sided valley, are the Butter Tubs, a series of limestone swallow-holes near the roadside, deep enough to be dangerous to fall down, yet shallow enough to allow the shade-loving ferns such as hart's-tongue to thrive in them. They can be easily viewed, but their rocky margins are slippery in wet weather. There is roadside parking and an explanatory notice-board.

Flat-topped Addlebrough is one of Wensleydale's best-known sights. Legend has it that it was once the home of a giant who had a fierce row with the devil, in which they both hurled huge boulders at each other

Wensleydale

Map Ref: SD8590 to SE1088

Of the major dales Wensleydale is the most pastoral and gentle, green and generously wooded. Even in its upper reaches above Hawes it never achieves the wildness of the lonely, exuberant beginnings of its neighbours to the north and south. During medieval times much of Wensleydale was owned by the Lords of Middleham and Bolton, the Abbots of Jervaulx and the Metcalfes of Nappa and it was not until the 16th and early 17th centuries that this large-scale land ownership broke down and the valley became more an area of yeomen-farmers. Good valley pastures and the subsequent improvement and enclosure of land along the hillsides resulted in increased dairying, and today's farming pattern is one in which this predominates, although higher up the dale sheep play an increasingly important part in the rural economy.

Wensleydale is the only dale in the National Park which has, at Bainbridge, a Roman fort. It also has two castles, Middleham and Bolton, two market towns, Leyburn and Hawes, two main feeder valleys, Bishopdale and Coverdale, two important waterfalls, Aysgarth and Hardraw, two National Park Centres, Aysgarth and Hawes, and two roads up the valley.

The main road, A684, traverses the whole length of the dale as part of an important link between the A1 and M6, making it particularly popular with visitors. Beyond Wensley it keeps to the southern side and passes through West Witton, Aysgarth and Bainbridge, to Hawes, while the northern road links Redmire, Carperby and Askrigg. Bridges at Aysgarth and Bainbridge provide link roads, and the A684 continues as the only westbound route a mile

Wensleydale Cheese

The medieval **Abbots** of Jervaulx were probably responsible for introducing cheese-making to Wensleydale. The formula and method of manufacture have been handed down from one generation to another either by word of mouth or through practical instruction, only relatively recently have written recipes been used. Inevitably local variations have evolved, mainly in Coverdale, Swaledale and Teesdale, but the basic methods have remained the same.

The original cheese was made from ewes' milk, but by the 17th century Shorthorn cows were supplanting ewes as milk-producers, sheep being bred increasingly for the wool and mutton. Farmhouse cheeses of those days were pickled by salting in brine, and not until 1890 was dry salting introduced. Cheese-making was essentially a summer occupation on farms, largely the responsibility of farmers' wives and other womenfolk, and although some cheeses were for home consumption most went either to the local grocer or corn merchant, usually on the barter system.

At the end of the 19th century Edward Chapman, a Hawes corn and provision merchant, was the biggest local buyer of farmhouse cheeses, and in 1897 he decided to buy milk in bulk from the farms and manufacture the cheese himself. He established the first Wensleydale cheese factory, by Gayle Beck in Hawes, based on a daily intake of 200 gallons of milk. Soon, Alfred Rowntree followed the example and set up factories at Masham, Coverham and Thoralby, using milk from lower Wensleydale, Coverdale and Bishopdale.

In 1935 the newly formed Milk Marketing Board, which had earlier accepted marketing responsibility for the cheese, threatened to close the Hawes creamery, but the late Kit Calvert MBE, of Hawes, opposed this idea. Putting up some capital himself, and persuading local farmers to support him, he bought the factory,

Above left: At work in the creameries. Above right: An old fashioned cheese press

where he ran the cheese-making enterprise until his retirement in 1966. During those years a new creamery was opened at Hawes, and in 1964 a larger one at Kirkby Malzeard. Wensleydale cheese is now made at both these creameries together with the one at Coverham, enlarged and modernised. Between them they handle thousands of gallons of milk each day, turning out hundreds of tons of cheese annually. Although all sizes of cheeses can now be bought in sealed polythene packs the industry still provides cheeses wrapped and matured in the traditional way that has been so successful over the years. Wensleydale cheese can reasonably claim to have 700 years of experience in its manufacture.

beyond Hawes. On the south side Coverdale and Bishopdale are corridors through the hills to Wharfedale, while from Hawes North Yorkshire's highest road crosses Fleet Moss into Langstrothdale. The B6255 leads southwards to Ribble Head or Dentdale, the Butter Tubs Pass is to the north of Hawes on a minor road leading into upper Swaledale, and moorland roads from Askrigg and Redmire are additional ways over into Wensleydale's northern neighbour.

Wensleydale's villages possess marked individuality – Castle Bolton, Carperby, Askrigg, West Witton and Thornton Rust being markedly linear, Wensley, Redmire, West Burton and Bainbridge delightfully grouped round well-kept greens. Hillsides show a 'stepped' profile, the result of differential weathering of the Yoredale strata, but it is the long limestone scars which are most significant. Penhill and Addlebrough on the south side show familiar plateau summits, the former more easily accessible, and climbable from West Witton Moor. Tracks made by quarrymen, lead-miners, packhorses, and even Romans encourage easy exploration away from roads, but the more gregarious-minded will find their pleasures at Aysgarth, Semer Water, and in the market towns of this greenest of Dales. Visitors are catered for by a good range of accommodation, and Wensleydale, from just below Leyburn to above Hawes, has more facilities for camping and caravanning than the other dales.

The Butter Tubs, Wensleydale

Wensley

Map Ref: 87SE0989

A mile south-west of Leyburn this small village of 19th-century estate-style houses round a neat green gives its name to a broad and gracious valley. Scenically, Wensleydale starts here, with the hills along each side becoming more important in the landscape. Above Wensley livestock farming predominates; below are the first arable fields in the dale.

Wensley Church was built on the site of a former Anglo-Danish structure

For a century after 1202, when it received its charter, Wensley had the only market in the dale, and this continued to function until the 16th century, though on a decreasing scale as other markets were founded. Plague struck Wensley in 1563, and as the parish register of crops notes, 'This year nothing set down'. Some surviving villagers fled to higher ground at Leyburn, but Wensley revived a century later when Charles Powlett, who had married the daughter of the last Lord Scrope, became Duke of Bolton, built Bolton Hall in 1678, with Wensley the village at its gates. The present Bolton Hall is largely a 1902 rebuilding after a serious fire, but the shell of the 17th-century house survives. There are public footpaths through the park and woodlands of the Hall.

Wensley Church is one of the finest in the Dales. Much of it dates from around 1300 but the tower was rebuilt in 1719. The interior is

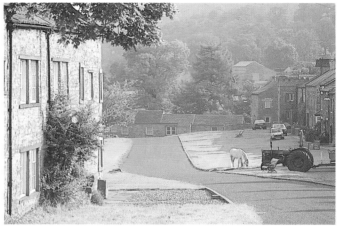

West Burton is an attractive village of pre Conquest date

remarkably rich in furnishings, with 17th-century box-pews, a reliquary, a poor-box, a two-decker pulpit, stalls and benches, and communion-rail. The Scrope family pew includes part of a fine Rood Screen which probably came from Easby Abbey at the Dissolution in 1535. There is also a banner of the Loyal Dales Volunteers who were raised against Napoleon, and traces of an early 14th-century wall painting.

AA recommends:
Hotels: Wensleydale Heifer Inn, 2-star, *tel.* Wensleydale 22322 (2 miles SW on A684 at West Witton)

West Burton

Map Ref: 86SE0186

Off Wensleydale, but not in the main valley West Burton encapsulates what are all the essential attributes of a village in the Dales. The B6160 Bishopdale road to Buckden in Wharfedale carefully turns away at a corner of the village which is thus conveniently left on no through road to anywhere. Modest houses and cottages of grey-brown stone border a long rectangular green whose focal-point is a stepped obelisk of 1820, which is neither a memorial

nor a market cross. West Burton never had a market, nor has it a church. Villagers worshipped, were baptised, married and buried, at Aysgarth – hence the number of old field-paths and tracks converging there from villages of lower Bishopdale. Most of West Burton's houses were miners' and quarrymen's properties, and although scarcely a single individual building is outstanding, the whole merits Conservation Area status. In setting, shape and appearance West Burton is memorable, with the bonus of a charming waterfall, Burton Force, by the lower end of the village.

Twin roads lead southward into Walden – not a dale by name, but a deeply-cut valley enclosed at its head by the great mass of Buckden Pike, 2302 feet. The western one ends at Kentucky and Walden Head, whence a rough track follows the beck and crosses the watershed into Wharfedale. The eastern valley road is shorter, ending near Low Dovescar. From Whiterow a well-defined grassy track climbs to former coal-pits on the moors and drops into Coverdale at Braidley and Horsehouse. Both roads up Walden pass 17th-century farms which are good examples of the characteristic long, narrow buildings of the Pennines.

Limekilns

L ike the miles of limestone walls which pattern the Dales' landscape the limekilns tend to be taken for granted, yet several hundred survive from the days when lime-burning was at its peak. By about

A Ribblehead limekiln

1760 a start had been made to enclose land on the moorland edge. After walling, it was burned, drained and limed. Huge quantities of lime were needed; there was abundant limestone, but this had to be burned so kilns were necessary, and it is the cave-like mouths of these which identify their location.

Limekilns are made of dry-stone masonry in the form of squat towers, flat or slightly bow-fronted, 12–20 feet across, about the same height, with a funnel-shaped lining of sandstone or brick, cylindrical in its upper part but tapering at the bottom to a narrow neck beneath which is the grate for collecting lime and ash, subsequently raked out from the hearth at the back of the kiln. Limekilns were usually sited at the foot of a limestone outcrop, so that broken lumps of quarried stone

could easily be fed into the top, together with alternate layers of coal, ideally obtained from small pits on the moors above. One part of coal to four of limestone would give a good burn, initiated by firing brushwood at the base, and kept charged by adding more limestone and coal, so that a continuous burn could last for 2–3 days, yielding 300 packhorse loads of 2½ cwts each. Four loads was a cartful, and an acre of land needed ten carts full. Many farms had their own kilns. Large kilns or small groups of kilns produced lime on a commercial basis, at fourpence a load. Most of the resultant lime was used to sweeten sour moorland soils and make good pasture; some was used in lime-mortar for Dales' buildings, and the use of limekilns lasted from 1760 to 1860.

Wharfedale

Map Ref: SD9278 to SE1945

Of all the dales' rivers the Wharfe is the most approachable, and from Bolton Abbey upwards to its headwaters of Cam Beck and Oughtershaw Beck over twenty miles away, the road up Wharfedale is never more than a couple of hundred yards from the river. Almost wholly in the Craven Pennines, Wharfedale's scenery is dominated by the Great Scar Limestone, and throughout the valley white scars of rock etch the hillsides, sometimes faintly, sometimes with dramatic effect as at Kilnsey Crag.

Anglian pioneers moving up the valley from the east during the 6th and 7th centuries established the pattern of village settlement recognised today – Bolton, Appletreewick, Hebden, Burnsall, Thorpe, Linton, Threshfield, Grassington, Conistone and Kettlewell. Tenth-century Norse settlers from west of the Pennines have given us the farm-hamlets of the upper dale beyond Buckden, itself a village on the edge of Norman hunting forest. In medieval times Fountains Abbey and Bolton Priory owned great estates in Wharfedale and on the surrounding limestone uplands the pattern of roads and green lanes evolved largely from them, together with the development of market roads and later of drove roads.

Above Burnsall in particular Wharfedale shows the palimpsest of the Enclosure Acts, mainly between 1780 and 1820 when the old common fields were broken up into rectangular pastures enclosed by hundreds of miles of limestone walls in the valley bottom and on the lower slopes of the hills. The memory of the

Part of the life-cycle in Wharfedale

great Cliffords lingers on in the ruins of Barden Tower, and around Bolton, following the Dissolution, Wharfedale became, eventually, the property of the Dukes of Devonshire, who have, by planting trees, imparted a lush, parkland character to this part of the valley. The Devonshires also revitalised and developed the vast lead-mining enterprises on Yarnbury Moor, above Grassington, but on the whole past industries – cornmilling and textiles – have left few discordant remains. Wharfedale is pre-eminently the sylvan dale, best appreciated from the miles of riverside and field paths, always recognisable from a car window.

From below Bolton Abbey two roads lead up the dale as far as Kettlewell, the better one, B6160, on the western side, but even this is narrow and winding. Every village

Below: Hundreds of miles of limestone walls were built in Wharfedale in the late 18th century. Right: Harebells growing in Wharfedale

has its own distinctive appeal, with Linton scoring heavily on account of its grouping round a green with a beck flowing down the centre. Grassington is an important, busy metropolis for the dale, with the charm of a village and the functions of a town – as well as good car-parking facilities. Beyond it, on the eastern side of the dale, Grass Wood is an important Nature Reserve, and at Kilnsey is a fishing and river-life Visitor Centre. Nearby is Littondale, with roads to Malham and Ribblesdale, while from Kettlewell a wild upland road crosses to Coverdale.

Wharfedale changes above Buckden, where the B6160 continues over to Bishopdale, but the valley itself narrows, changes its name to Langstrothdale, receives a benediction at Hubberholme church, and its beauty becomes more concentrated as the dale narrows, and road partners a clear river which chuckles over limestone ledges. Woods diminish, except for recent plantations above Beckermonds and Oughtershaw where the winding road climbs over the bleak, bare uplands into Wensleydale.

Directory

ANGLING

Most Dales rivers and tributaries with game fish are privately owned, and fishing permits can be bought locally, often at village pubs. Rod licences are issued by the appropriate water authorities who also allow game and coarse fishing on stretches of water under their control, and each authority publishes a descriptive leaflet.

For Rivers Ribble, Lune and Eden:
North West Water Authority
Rivers Division
PO Box 12
New Town House
Buttermarket Street
Warrington WA1 2QG
tel (0925) 53999

For Rivers Aire, Nidd, Swale, Ure and Wharfe:
Yorkshire Water Authority
Rivers Division
67 West Riding House
Albion Street
Leeds LS1 5AA
tel (0532) 448201
Malham Tarn, Semer Water, Kilnsey Park and Foster Beck Mill issue day tickets. See *Northern Anglers' Handbook* for details.

CAVES AND CAVING

The Dales is an area well-known for its caves and the Yorkshire Dales National Park contains the most important limestone countryside in Britain (see feature on page 12). For the experienced caver there is the opportunity to explore caves in their natural state. For the less dedicated underground visitor the Dales offer some delightful show-caves.

Ingleborough Cave Clapham *(off the A65 between Settle and Ingleton) tel* (04685) 242.
This show-cave is approximately one-third of a mile long with good footpaths all electrically lit. It contains fine examples of stalactites, stalagmites, fossils exposed in the roof and walls, and other interesting geological features. The cave is approached from the village of Clapham and is reached by either walking through the wooded Ingleborough Estate, or via a public footpath past Clapdale Farm. The cave is open daily Mar–Oct and part-time during the remainder of the year. Guided tours are available.

Stump Cross Caverns Greenhow Hill *(on the B6265 between Grassington and Pateley Bridge) tel* (0423) 711042.
Some of Britain's finest stalactite and stalagmite formations are shown to wonderful effect by electric coloured lighting.

Whernside Manor Cave and Fell Centre Dent *tel* (05875) 213.
This is the only specialist caving centre in the country.
One mile from Dent, Whernside Manor is ideal for exploring the three hundred or so caves within a fifteen mile radius. The centre offers a complete range of courses in caving and pot-holing including day visits for the beginner. These involve basic instruction in caving together with a visit to a local cave and are available throughout the year.

White Scar Caves Ingleton *tel* (0468) 41244.
The White Scar Caves are fully equipped with footpaths and floodlights so they can be seen by visitors in comfort. Besides carrying a powerful stream through their length, White Scar Caves also have spectacular waterfalls, tall passages, classically revealed geological features and beautiful stalactites and stalagmites. Open daily with regular, organised tours.

CHURCHES

DENT, ST ANDREW'S Founded in Norman times, much of the present building is 15th century, though some Norman decoration remains. The church features a beautiful unique chancel floor made from the fine Dent marble.

The Yorkshire Dales boasts many caves dripping with stalactites and stalagmites

HORTON IN RIBBLESDALE, ST OSWALD'S The present church is as old as the reign of Henry I (1100–1135), and the rugged nature of this building is perfectly complemented by its rugged setting. Parts of the building have a distinct and disturbing lean to the south.

HUBBERHOLME, ST MICHAEL'S Originally a forest chapel, built on an Anglo-Norse burial site. The tower and south door are Norman and the rood loft is extremely rare. The more recent additions to the church harmonise with the older aspects of it.

KIRKBY MALHAM, ST MICHAEL THE ARCHANGEL Commonly known as the Cathedral of the Dales, this spacious 15th-century church testifies to more turbulent times. There are unusual niches in the western most piers of the nave which once held statues, presumably removed by Cromwell or his contemporaries. The invasion beam on the inside of the south door reminds visitors of those times.

LINTON-IN-CRAVEN, ST MICHAEL AND ALL ANGELS The simple exterior of this church with its squat bell-turret belies the pleasures to be discovered inside.

LONG PRESTON, ST MARY THE VIRGIN One of the few churches in the area to be mentioned in the Domesday Book. A church of some kind existed on this site long before the Norman Conquest but most of the present church dates from the late 14th and early 15th centuries. A feature of the church is a Saxon tombstone built into the west wall of the porch.

CRAFT WORKSHOPS

Many villages, and most of the small market towns in the Yorkshire Dales have shops which display and sell items of local crafts. Additionally there are a number of potteries and craft workshops where visitors can watch items being made, as well as seeing good displays of craft products. The following list includes many, but not necessarily all, of the potteries and craft workshops in the area, given on a geographical basis.

SWALEDALE

Reeth: *The Pot Shop*, where Carol Bearpark has a comprehensive selection of domestic, hand-thrown pottery, made by her husband Martin at the studio in Low Row (near the Punchbowl Hotel) higher up Swaledale. Open daily 10–5.30
Mews Crafts, behind the Green, concentrates on hand-knitted goods, soft toys, embroidery, and has a small range of pottery made at Marrick.
Muker: *Swaledale Woollens* must be mentioned because of the wide range of sweaters, ties, tweeds, made locally from Swaledale and Herdwick wool. Open daily.

WENSLEYDALE

Middleham: *The Old School Arts Workshop tel* Wensleydale (0969) 23056 is an independent Arts Centre housed in the Victorian Gothic-style former school building opposite the castle. Sculptor Peter Hibbard and his wife Judith have restored it as a residential study centre for sculpture and the visual arts. They offer activity holiday courses, and, during the season, one-day courses (including lunch). These give holiday visitors staying in the area the chance to spend a day in a studio. Disabled people can participate in arts courses, but not sculpture. Regular exhibitions are displayed in the Gallery, changing every five or six weeks. Open during the season 10–5. Closed out of season Monday and Friday.

Leyburn: *Swineside Ceramics,* formerly at West Scrafton, now operates from a new COSIRA factory unit in Bedale Road, where domestic pottery is produced by slip-casting method. Visitors are welcome daily, 9–5.

West Witton: *West Witton Pottery,* in the centre of the village on the main A684 road up the dale. Paul Green makes and shows a full range of stoneware for kitchen and home. The pots are all oven-proof. Commissions are welcomed and the pottery is open daily 10–5, except Wednesday.

Aysgarth: *Aysgarth Pottery* is housed in a converted barn in the middle of this main road village, half a mile above the waterfalls. Visitors are invited to view the work in progress through the downstairs windows and see the finished products displayed in the old hay-loft above. The wide range of useful and decorative stoneware is finished in fresh pastel colours, and Terracotta planters for home or garden use are also made. Charles Boyce and Lucy Craven open the pottery daily, 9.30–5.30, Mar–Oct.

Thoralby: Brian Oliver runs the *Bishopdale Forge,* where visitors can see a good range of decorative wrought-ironwork made in the traditional way. The forge is open daily 10–5, including Sunday, from Easter to the end of September. Commissioned work is undertaken.

Hawes: At the *Wensleydale Pottery tel* Hawes (09697) 594 (through the arch by the second-hand bookshop) Simon Shaw makes and displays high-fired glazed stoneware for the home, with cheese dishes for the 1lb Wensleydale Cheeses a speciality. Gardenware is also manufactured. Open daily, except Sunday 9.30—6.

Hawes Ropeworks. Rope making has been carried out in Hawes since about 1840, initially at Gate House, a former tollhouse, on the Ingleton road, and since 1922 at the present premises at Town Foot, near the entrance to the Station Yard. Peter and Ruth Annison took over the rope-making business in 1975 since when it has steadily expanded, so that

Wrought ironwork in the making at Thoralby's Bishopdale Forge

in 1981 the original wooden shed used for rope-making for nearly 60 years had to be replaced with longer indoor ropewalk.

Visitors can watch rope being made, and the longest that can be made on the premises is about 100 feet. Most ropes, however, are short – 6 feet for leading reins, 11 feet for halters for cattle and horses. High-quality cotton is still used for ropes which need to be soft to the touch, but the introduction of man-made fibres offers a greater choice of raw materials, with properties making them suitable for outdoor agricultural use. In the growing range of rope products made at the Hawes Ropeworks are bannister and barrier ropes, bell ropes, clothes lines, hammocks, garden twine, macramé items, picture cord, rope belts, dolls and ladders, skipping ropes and wagon ropes. Visitors are welcomed, and the Ropeworks is open daily, except Sunday.

GARSDALE

Aisgill Country Crafts, three miles along the B6259 north of the 'Moorcock' specialises in Jacob/ Shetland woollen products and hand-crafted walking sticks. Spinning demonstrations are given and there is spinning equipment for sale.

DENTDALE

Dent: At their studio by the fountain *John and Eliza Forder* exhibit landscape, caving, and portrait photographs, together with sepia prints from ½ plate negatives of old Dent, c1890–1900. Loose black and white prints are for sale. Open daily. *Dents Craft Centre,* west of Dent on the Sedbergh road. Displays and sells a wide range of crafts products made by Brian and Matty Bradley and their craft workers, using wood, clay, wool, paper. Specialities include the recycling of old bobbins of all sizes into many decorative items – engines, hour-glasses, cotton-reel holders, candlesticks, and the recycling of old printing blocks. There is a resident potter. Open daily, Easter to Christmas.

SEDBERGH

At *Pennine Tweeds,* Fairfield Mill, on A684, Mr & Mrs David Douglas are weavers of fine quality tweeds, Mohair, travel and knee rugs. Visitors are welcome, and the showroom is open daily, and Saturday mornings.

Brackensghyll Pottery, Black Lane, where David Alban makes bright, clean earthenware in a variety of colours, with a good range of bowls, pots for house plants, and flower arrangers' pieces. Open daily, 10–5, except Thursday and Sunday.

CLAPHAM

At the *Dales Pottery,* Peter and Cynthia Strong concentrate on hand-made earthenware for the kitchen and garden. Using clay obtained locally they supply the area with a wide range of household and horticultural vessels, made in traditional styles that have changed little over 250 years. All items are guaranteed to withstand frost and oven temperatures. Open daily.

LITTONDALE

Litton: *Littondale Pottery* is where Ron and Margaret Walker specialise in ceramic sculpture, and display a range of decorative models. Open daily, except Sunday.

GOLF
BENTHAM GOLF CLUB, Robin Lane, *tel* (0468) 61018 (9 hole course) is amid meadowland with glorious views.

RICHMOND GOLF CLUB, Bend Hagg, *tel* (0748) 2457 (18 hole course) mostly parkland, good facilities.

SETTLE GOLF CLUB, Duckhaw Brow, Giggleswick, *tel* (07292) 2617 (9 hole course) is set in picturesque parkland.

SKIPTON GOLF CLUB, on by-pass off Grassington Rd, *tel* (0756) 3922 (18 hole course) offers panoramic views.

CALENDAR OF EVENTS

April
Three Peaks Race

May
Hardraw Band Contest *(Hawes)*
'Fellsman' Hike *(Ingleton)*
Arkengarthdale Sports and Sheep Show
Tan Hill Show *(last Thursday)*
Swaledale Festival

June
Pen-y-ghent Race and Gala, Horton
Grassington Festival
Hawes Sports and Gala

August
Grassington Exhibition
Malham Show
Reeth Show
Wensleydale Agricultural Show, Leyburn *(Bank Holiday Saturday)*
Burnsall Sports *(third Saturday)*
Hebden Sports *(Bank Holiday Monday)*
Upper Wharfedale Agricultural Show
Kilnsey Show *(Tuesday after Bank Holiday Monday)*
West Witton Feast and the Burning of Bartle *(Saturday nearest 24 Aug)*

September
Swaledale Agricultural Show, Muker
Horton Show
Moorcock Show, Lunds
Nidderdale Agricultural Show, Pateley Bridge *(Monday nearest 20 Sep)*
Three Peaks Cycle-cross

The exact dates vary slightly each year, so details should be checked at Information Centres.

Main picture: The Union Jack flutters
proudly on Whernside's summit during
April's Three Peaks Race

top: Swaledale rams for sale at Tan Hill
Show in May
centre: September brings the Three Peaks
Cycle-cross
bottom: The hills are alive with the
sound of Hardraw brass band contest

MUSEUMS

AYSGARTH The Yorkshire Museum of Carriages and Horse Drawn Vehicles, Yore Mill. Carriages, coaches, vehicles and other impedimenta used by the country squire and his estate. Open most days Easter–Oct. Small charge.

Bronze-age arrowhead in Grassington Museum

GRASSINGTON Grassington Museum, The Square. Portrays life in upper Wharfedale with special reference to farming, local industries and trades, veterinary equipment, prehistoric finds, and has a good mineral collection. Open afternoons Apr–Oct. Small charge.

HAWES Upper Dales Folk Museum, Station Yard. Displays a wide range of exhibits illustrating pastoral life in the Dales – farming, local crafts and trades, lead-mining, veterinary appliances. Based on the Marie Hartley and Joan Ingilby collection. Open Easter–30 Sep. Small charge.

PATELEY BRIDGE Nidderdale Museum, Old Council Offices. Fascinating range of exhibits housed in former Victorian workhouse, illustrating local life and history, with many unique items. Temporary collections also displayed. Open afternoons, Easter–Oct. Small charge.

REETH Swaledale Folk Museum, Reeth Green. Shows agricultural life, lead mining, social conditions in bygone days. Open daily Easter–Sep. Small charge.

RICHMOND Richmondshire Museum, Ryders Wynd. Local history display includes evolution of the town, farming, lead-mining, models, photographs. Open afternoons 29 May–23 Sep. Small charge.
Georgian Theatre and Theatre Museum, Victoria Road. Unique Georgian theatre and adjoining museum – handbills, playbills, costumes, photographs. Guided tours of auditorium and backstage. Open afternoons May–Sep, plus Saturday and Bank Holiday Monday mornings. Charge made.
Green Howards Regimental Museum, Trinity Church.

Memorabilia of this famous Yorkshire Regiment 1688 to modern times. Apr–Oct, weekdays. Charge made.

SETTLE Museum of North Craven Life, Victoria Street. Interpretive displays on the landscape, settlement, farming and other aspects of North Craven life. May–Jun, Saturday and Sunday afternoons. Jul–Sep, afternoons (except Monday). Small charge.

SKIPTON Craven Museum, Town Hall, High Street. Good collection includes geology, natural history, local history, archaeology. Open daily, weekdays, Sunday afternoons, Apr–Sep. Admission free.

OPEN GARDENS

Although the Yorkshire Dales is not noted for stately mansions or fine grounds, a number of gardens are opened during summer weekends, usually in aid of some charity or local organisation. In addition, the beautiful gardens and grounds of Parcevall Hall, a Diocesan conference centre, are open daily, Apr–Oct, 10am to 6pm. Parcevall Hall is near Appletreewick, in Wharfedale.

RAIL & ROAD

Dales Rail Apart from the National Park Centres and Offices, information about Dales Rail can be obtained from: Dales Rail, Metro House, West Parade, Wakefield, WF1 1NS.
British Rail Passenger train stations are located at Skipton, Gargrave, Hellifield, Long Preston, Giggleswick, Settle, Clapham, Bentham, Ilkley and Oxenholme.
Bus Services Timetables of bus services are available at National Park Centres (see box on page 59).

RIDING AND TREKKING

Why not explore the beauty and remoteness of the Upper Dales on horseback? Full and half-day treks are available together with weekly trekking holidays. Riding and trekking lessons are offered at the following establishments:
Austwick: *Rawlinshaw Farm* Grid Reference SD 781 672 *tel* Settle (07292) 3214

Coverdale: *Brookside Cottage, Horsehouse.* Grid Reference SE 048 812 *tel* Wensleydale (0969) 40611

Gargrave: *Newton Grange, Bank Newton.* Grid Reference SD 913 524. *tel* Gargrave (075678) 243

Hawes: *Sedbusk Trekking Centre, Sedbusk.* Grid Reference SD 883 912 *tel* Hawes (09697) 403

Wharfedale: *Kilnsey Trekking Centre, Homestead Farmhouse, Conistone.* Grid Reference SD 981 675 *tel* Grassington (0756) 752861

Settle Market brightens Tuesdays

SHOPPING: MARKET DAYS

(List includes some towns on the fringe of the Dales)

Appleby	Saturday
Barnard Castle	Wednesday
Hawes	Tuesday
Ingleton	Friday
Kirkby Stephen	Monday
Kirkby Lonsdale	Thursday
Leyburn	Friday
Knaresborough	Wednesday
Richmond	Saturday
Ripon	Thursday
Sedbergh	Wednesday
Settle	Tuesday
Skipton	Monday,

Wednesday, Friday, Saturday

THEATRE

Richmond The Georgian Theatre has now been given permission by HM The Queen to call itself the Royal Georgian Theatre.
The grey stone building resembles a barn more than anything else, but to step through its doorway is to enter a bygone age. Scarcely changed from the late 18th century is the tiny paybox or the narrow flights of stone steps leading to boxes bearing illustrious names; Shakespeare, Goldsmith, Sheridan and Dryden among them. Beyond the boxes more steps lead to the gallery which still retains its barracking board, kicked by the feet of Georgian audiences. Below, in the stepped pit, the audience views the stage almost at touching distance. Red stage curtains match the canvas behind the boxes; delicate Georgian greens decorate doors and panels. The seating may not be as comfortable as that in modern theatres, but an audience of about 250 can enjoy and appreciate plays, recitals and 'one-man shows' presented regularly throughout the year, for the essence of the Royal Georgian Theatre at Richmond is that it is not just a unique museum but a living theatre, fulfilling the functions for which it was built by Samuel Butler in 1788. Names as famous as those of his time now grace the playbills, and for today's actors and actresses a performance here is a special event.

YORKSHIRE DALES

Atlas

The following pages contain a legend, key map and atlas of the Yorkshire Dales, two circular motor tours and sixteen planned walks in the Dales countryside.

Above: Swaledale rams grazing at Cross Keys, Cautley

Yorkshire Dales Legend

GRID REFERENCE SYSTEM

The map references used in this book are based on the Ordnance Survey National Grid. correct to within **1000 metres** They comprise two letters and four figures, and are preceded by the atlas page number.

Thus the reference for Hawes appears **84 SD 8789**

84 is the atlas page number

SD identifies the major (100km) grid square concerned (see diag)

TOURIST INFORMATION (All Scales)

Ă	Camp Site		Nature reserve
⚑	Caravan Site	☆	Other tourist feature
ℹ	Information Centre		Preserved railway
P	Parking Facilities		Racecourse
☀	Viewpoint		Wildlife park
✕	Picnic site		Museum
⚑	Golf course or links	m	Nature or forest trail
	Castle	m	Ancient monument
	Cave	▦	Places of interest
	Country park	☏	Telephones: public or motoring organisations
	Garden	PC	Public Convenience
	Historic house	▲	Youth Hostel

⊕ **Mountain Rescue Post** with telephone and supervisor

◆ ◆ ◇ ◇ Waymarked Path / Long Distance Path

	78/79	80/81
82/83	84/85	86/87
88/89	90/91	92/93
	94/95	96/97

ORIENTATION

True North
At the centre of the area is 10'E of Grid North

Magnetic North
At the centre of the area is about 6½°W of Grid North in 1986 decreasing by about ½° in three years

8789 locates the lower left-hand corner of the kilometre grid square in which Hawes appears

87 can be found along the bottom edge of the page, reading W to E

89 can be found along the right hand side of the page, reading S to N

ATLAS 1:63,360 or 1" to 1 MILE

ROADS & PATHS Not necessarily rights of way

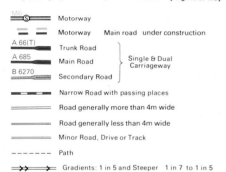

M6	Motorway
	Motorway Main road under construction
A 66(T)	Trunk Road
A 685	Main Road — Single & Dual Carriageway
B 6270	Secondary Road
	Narrow Road with passing places
	Road generally more than 4m wide
	Road generally less than 4m wide
	Minor Road, Drive or Track
	Path
	Gradients: 1 in 5 and Steeper 1 in 7 to 1 in 5

GENERAL FEATURES

Ă	Radio or TV mast		Quarry
⬥	Church { with tower		Spoil Heap or Refuse Tip
⬥	or { with spire		
+	Chapel { without tower or spire		Woods
○	Chimney or Tower		Orchard
⊘	Glasshouse		
⬛	Bus or Coach Station		Park or Ornamental Grounds
△	Triangulation Pillar		
Ⓧ	Windmill	×—×—×	Electricity Transmission Line
Ⓣ	Windpump	> — -> — ->	Pipe Line

RAILWAYS

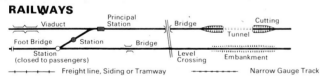

Viaduct	Principal Station	Bridge
		Cutting
Foot Bridge	Station	Tunnel
Station (closed to passengers)	Bridge	Level Crossing Embankment
	Freight line, Siding or Tramway	Narrow Gauge Track

ABBREVIATIONS

P	Post Office
PH	Public House
MP	Mile Post
MS	Mile Stone
LC	Level crossing
LDP	Long Distance Path
CH	Club House
TH	Town Hall, Guildhall or equivalent
PC	Public Convenience (in rural areas)

WATER FEATURES

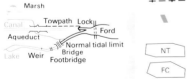

Marsh

Canal Towpath Lock
Aqueduct Ford
Normal tidal limit
Lake Weir Bridge Footbridge

BOUNDARIES

+—+—	National	—·—·—	County
	National Park	+·+·+	District
NT	National Trust	NT	always open
		NT	opening restricted
FC	Forestry Commission		Pedestrians only -observe local signs

ANTIQUITIES

VILLA	Roman	Castle	Non-Roman
✗	Battlefield (with date)		
✿	Tumulus		
+	Site of Antiquity		

PUBLIC RIGHTS OF WAY

··········	Footpath	—·+·+·+·—	Road used as a Public Path
— — — —	Bridleway	·+·+·+·+·	Byway open to all traffic

Public rights of way indicated by these symbols have been derived from Definitive Maps as amended by later enactments or instruments held by Ordnance Survey on 1st October 1984 and are shown subject to the limitations imposed by the scale of mapping.

The representation in this atlas of any other road, track or path is no evidence of the existence of a right of way.

Danger Area   MOD Ranges in the area. Danger! Observe warning notices

HEIGHTS & ROCK FEATURES

outcrop   cliff   650
600   scree

Contours are at 10 metres vertical interval

·144 Heights are to the nearest metre above mean sea level

Heights shown close to a triangulation pillar refer to the station height at ground level and not necessarily to the summit

TOURS 1:250,000 or ¼" to 1 MILE

ROADS Not necessarily rights of way

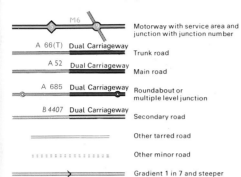

M6	Motorway with service area and junction with junction number
A 66(T) Dual Carriageway	Trunk road
A 52 Dual Carriageway	Main road
A 685 Dual Carriageway	Roundabout or multiple level junction
B 4407 Dual Carriageway	Secondary road
	Other tarred road
	Other minor road
	Gradient 1 in 7 and steeper

RAILWAYS

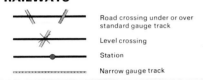

	Road crossing under or over standard gauge track
	Level crossing
	Station
	Narrow gauge track

WATER FEATURES

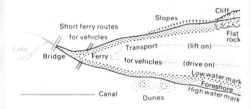

Lake, Bridge, Ferry, Short ferry routes for vehicles, Transport for vehicles (lift on) (drive on), Slopes, Cliff, Flat rock, Low water mark, Foreshore, High water mark, Canal, Dunes

ANTIQUITIES

	Native fortress
- - - - -	Roman road (course of)
Castle •	Other antiquities
CANOVIVM •	Roman antiquity

GENERAL FEATURES

	Buildings
	Wood
⊕	Civil aerodrome (with custom facilities)
Ⱦ	Radio or TV mast
	Lighthouse
☎	Telephones public or motoring organisations

RELIEF

Feet	Metres	
		.274
		Heights in feet above mean sea Level
3000	914	
2000	610	
1400	427	
1000	305	Contours at 200 ft intervals
600	183	
200	61	
0	0	To convert feet to metres multiply by 0.3048

WALKS 1:25,000 or 2½" to 1 MILE

ROADS AND PATHS Not necessarily rights of way

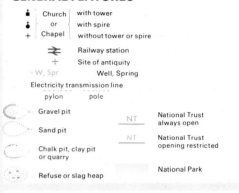

A 31(T)	Trunk road
A 35	Main road
B 3074	Secondary road
A 35	Dual carriageway
	Road generally over 4m wide
	Road generally under 4m wide
>>> >	Gradient: 20% (1 in 5) and steeper 14% (1 in 7) to 20% (1 in 5)
· · · · · · · ·	Path

- - - - - Permitted path and bridleway	Paths and bridleways along which landowners have permitted public use but which are not public rights of way. The agreement may be withdrawn.
Access Land ↗ Access Point	Land open to the public by permission of the owner

GENERAL FEATURES

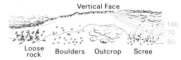

Church or Chapel	with tower
	with spire
	without tower or spire

⇌	Railway station
✛	Site of antiquity
· W, Spr	Well, Spring

Electricity transmission line
pylon   pole

	Gravel pit
	Sand pit
	Chalk pit, clay pit or quarry
	Refuse or slag heap
NT	National Trust always open
NT	National Trust opening restricted
	National Park

HEIGHTS AND ROCK FEATURES

Contours are at 10 metres vertical interval

50	Determined	ground survey
285 ·	by	air survey

Surface heights are to the nearest metre above mean sea level Heights shown close to a triangulation pillar refer to the station height at ground level and not necessarily to the summit

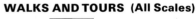

Vertical Face

Loose rock   Boulders   Outcrop   Scree

100
70
50

PUBLIC RIGHTS OF WAY

Public rights of way shown on this Atlas may not be evident on the ground

- - - - - -	Public Paths	Footpath
- - - - - -		Bridleway
+++++++	By-way open to all traffic	
‡-‡-‡-‡	Road used as a public path	

Public rights of way indicated have been derived from Definitive Maps as amended by later enactments or instruments held by Ordnance Survey between 1st April 1984 and 1st July 1984 and are shown subject to the limitations imposed by the scale of mapping.

The representation on this map of any other road, track or path is no evidence of the existence of a right of way.

WALKS AND TOURS (All Scales)

7 👣	Start point of walk
→	Route of walk
▬▬	Line of Walk
- - - -	Alternative route
2 🚗	Start point of tour
⇒	Route of tour
▬▬	Featured tour

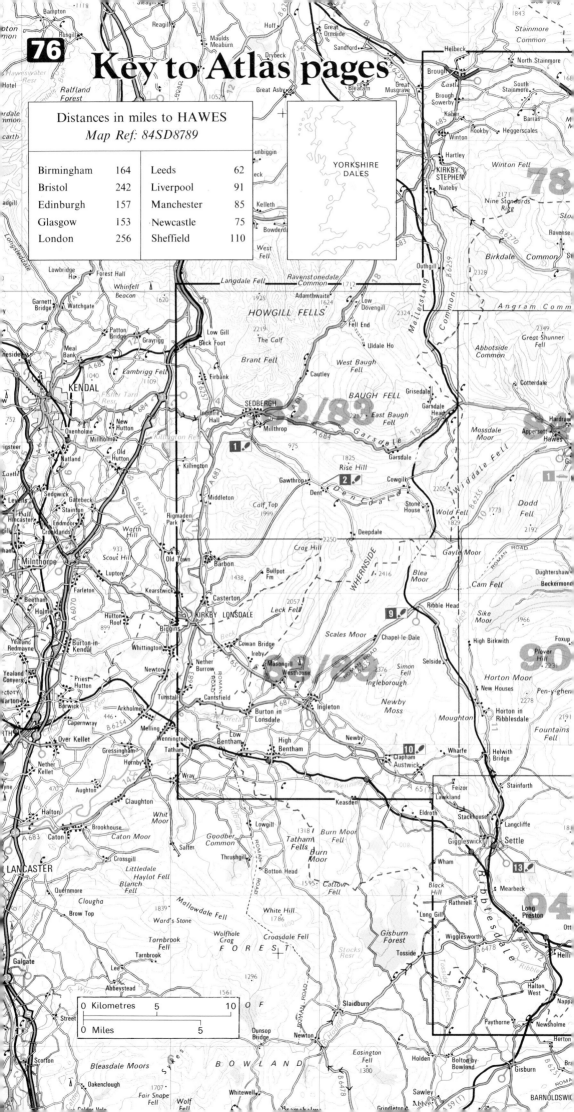

Key to Atlas pages

76

Distances in miles to HAWES
Map Ref: 84SD8789

Birmingham	164	Leeds	62
Bristol	242	Liverpool	91
Edinburgh	157	Manchester	85
Glasgow	153	Newcastle	75
London	256	Sheffield	110

YORKSHIRE DALES

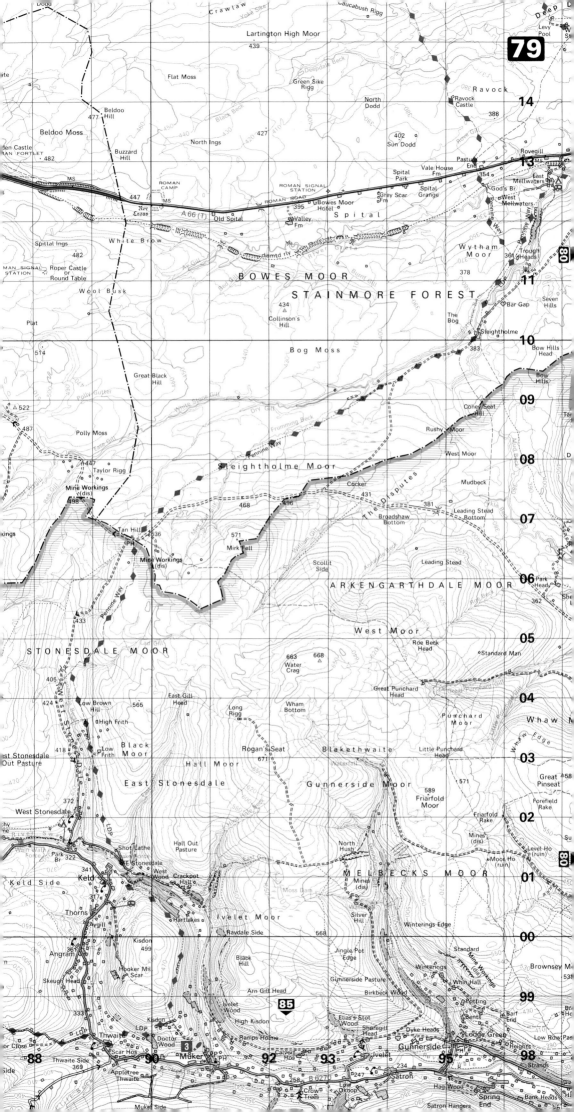

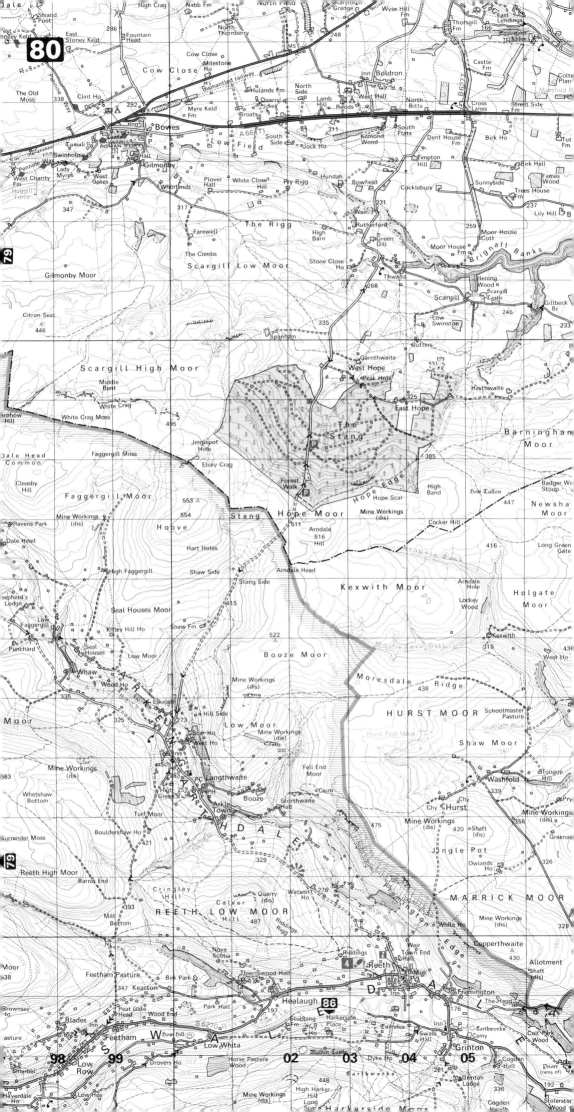

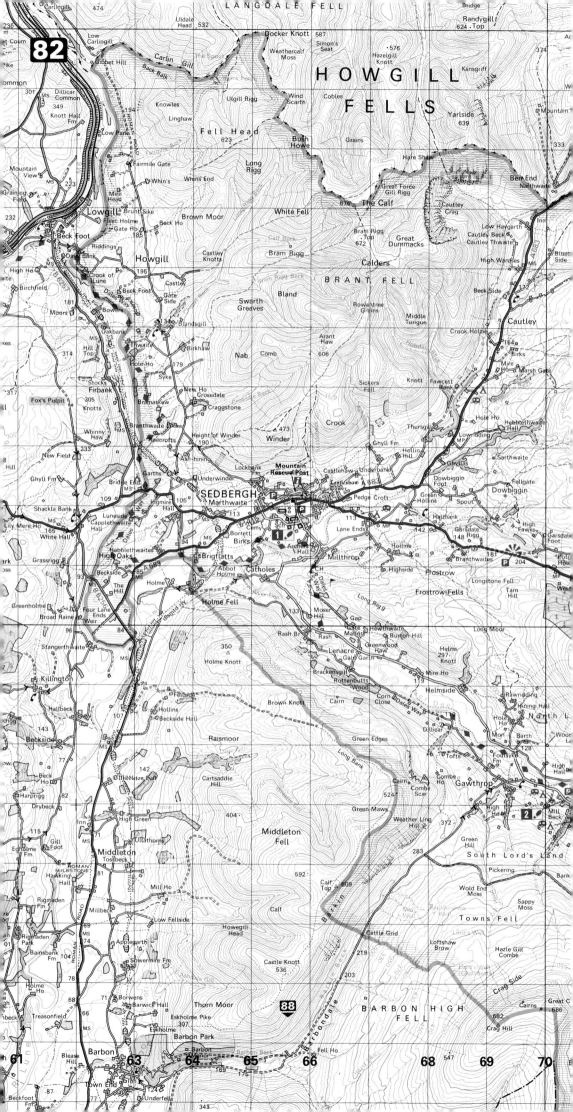

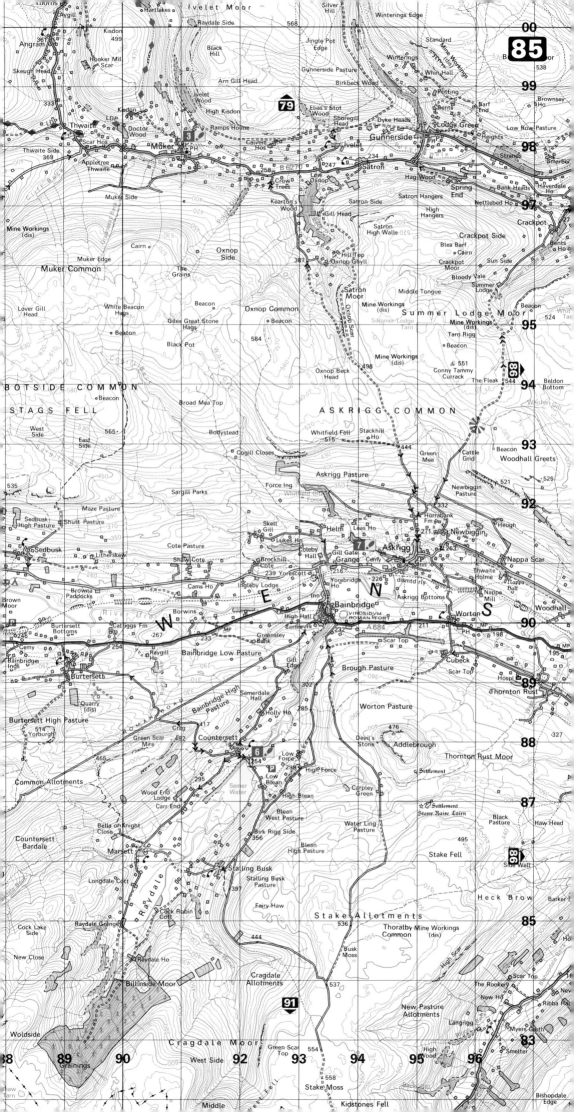

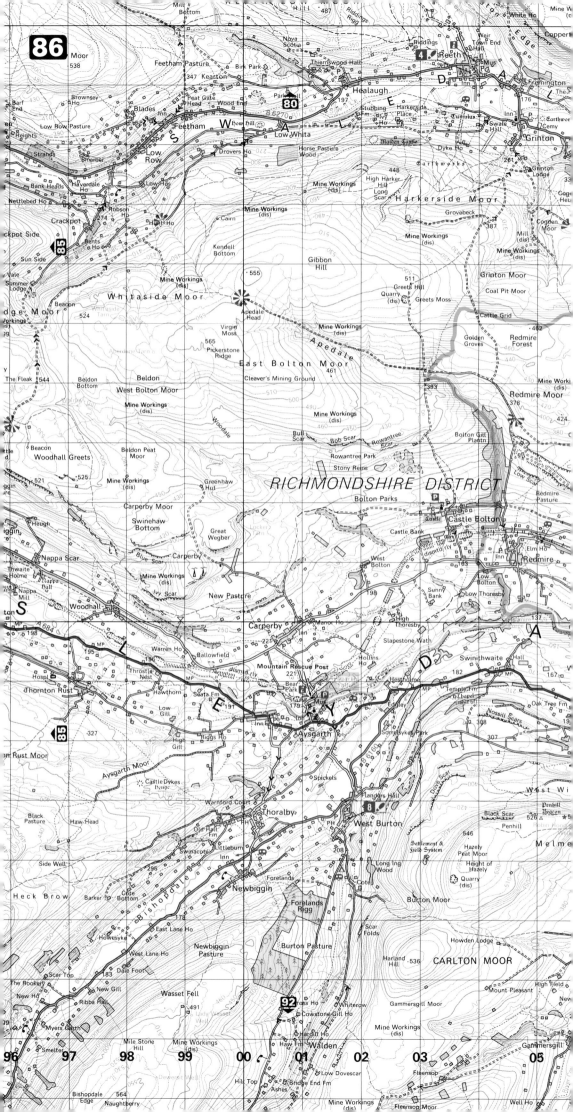

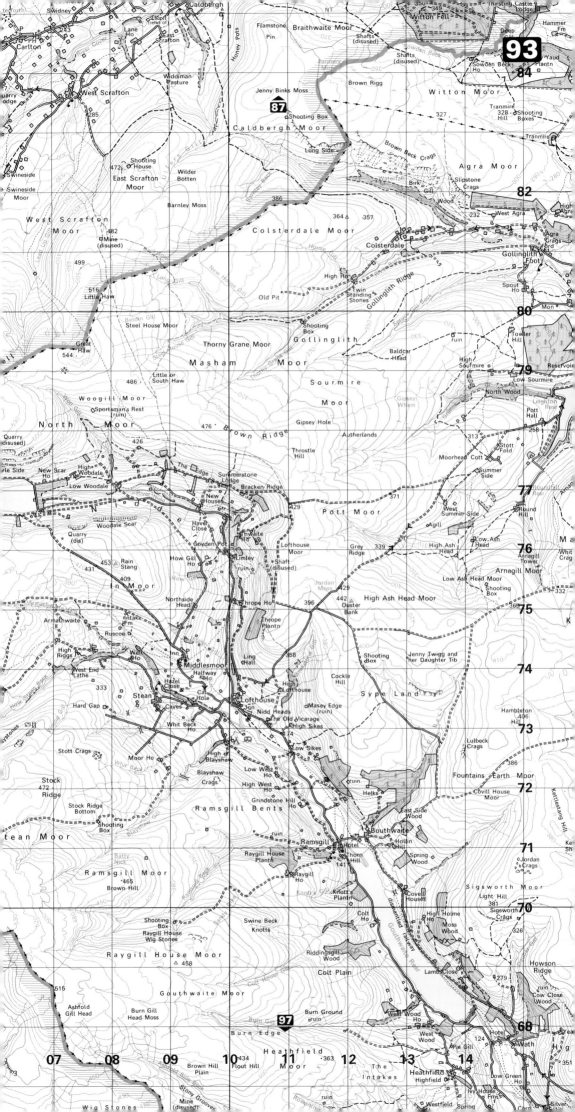

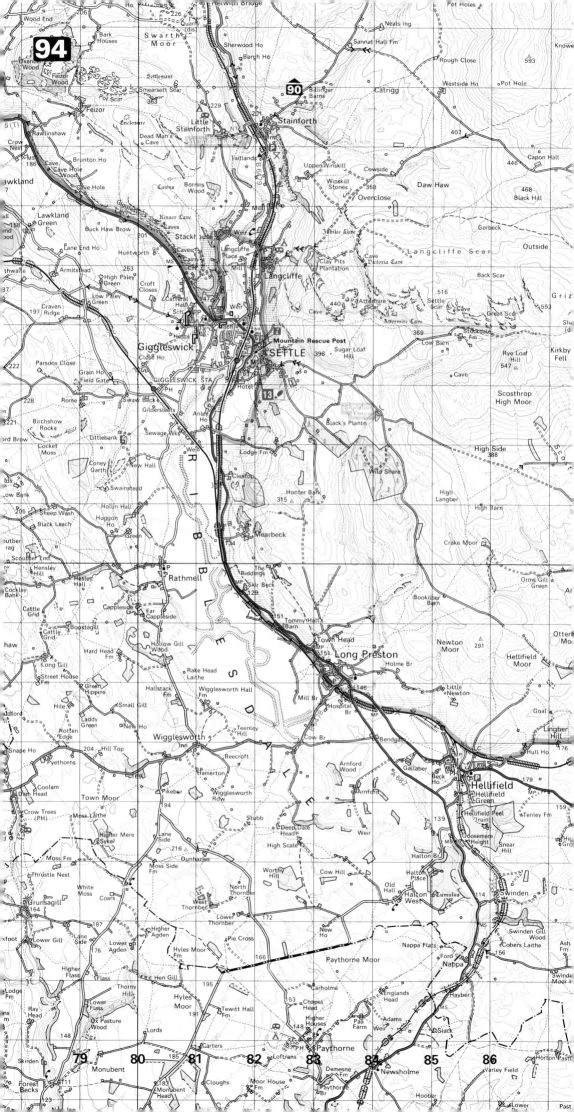

TOUR 1
57 MILES

Falls, Fells and Fortress

The bustling market town of Hawes is the start point for a tour which passes through Langstrothdale, and much of Wensleydale. It visits several waterfalls as well as the historic village of Castle Bolton, where Mary, Queen of Scots was imprisoned in the 16th century, Arkengarthdale, the most northerly Pennine Dale in Yorkshire and the famous Butter Tubs Pass.

The drive starts from Hawes (see page 44), the friendly market town for upper Wensleydale. The Yorkshire Dales National Park Centre is housed in the former station yard and visitors are welcome to call there for information about all parts of the Dales. Shops and amenities in the town are good, and there is ample parking.

Leave by the Sedbergh road, A684, and near the end of the main street turn left on to an unclassified road, signed Gayle and Kettlewell. Shortly cross the Duerley Beck (at Gayle) and follow a steep ascent through Sleddale. Fells rise to over 2000 ft on either side before reaching the summit where there is a good viewpoint at 1934 ft – this being the highest road in North Yorkshire.

A long descent is then made into the valley of Oughtershaw Beck. Beyond the hamlet of Oughtershaw follow the Kettlewell road alongside the river and enter Langstrothdale to reach the George Inn at Hubberholme. Here keep forward and continue to the Upper Wharfedale village of Buckden on the edge of Norman hunting forest. Turn left on to the B6160, signed Aysgarth, and climb out of the valley to over 1300 ft along the Kidstones Pass. A descent is then made into Bishopsdale to reach the edge of West Burton (see page 66). Here turn left, then branch on to an unclassified road (still signed Aysgarth). In 3/4 mile turn left on to the A684, and 1/4 mile further turn right on to an unclassified road, signed Aysgarth Force.
On the steep descent the drive passes the Yorkshire Museum of Carriages and Horse-Drawn Vehicles before crossing the River Ure. After a short distance there is a Yorkshire Dales National Park Centre (on the left) which provides a convenient car park in order to explore the nearby Aysgarth Force waterfall. Facilities for the disabled make it possible for visitors in wheelchairs to view the Lower Falls with ease.

Continue with the unclassified road and in 3/4 mile turn right, signed Castle Bolton, and enter Carperby (see page 38). Two miles farther turn left for Castle Bolton (see page 38). The impressive 14th-century stronghold here was once the prison of Mary, Queen of Scots. She and about twenty servants spent several months here in the troubled 16th century.

From this picturesque village follow the Reeth/Redmire road for 3/4 mile, then at the T-junction turn left, signed Grinton and Reeth. A long climb is then made on to the lonely Redmire and Grinton Moors. After the summit at over 1500 ft there are fine views on the descent into Swaledale.

Near the foot of the hill turn left to reach Grinton (see page 44). Here turn left on to the B6270 and cross the River Swale to Reeth (see page 57). The small Swaledale village, formerly a lead-mining centre, stands at the confluence of Arkle Beck and the River Swale. Its superb setting makes it a popular stopping place for visitors in summer.

At the Buck Hotel turn right on to the unclassified Langthwaite road and climb above the valley slopes of Arkengarthdale. Half a mile beyond Langthwaite keep forward, signed Tan Hill. The drive then crosses the desolate Arkengarthdale Moor for 7 1/2 miles to reach the Tan Hill Inn. At 1732 ft, this isolated hostelry on the route of the Pennine Way footpath is reputed to be the highest inn in England.

At the Inn turn left (no sign) and follow a moorland road to enter West Stones Dale. Later there is a steep descent, with hairpin bends, before crossing the River Swale and turning left on to the B6270 to reach the edge of Keld (see page 48).

To visit the waterfall of Kisdon Force enter the village and follow the signs. Continue along the B6270 to Thwaite (see page 64). Beyond this hamlet turn right on to an unclassified road, signed Hawes, and ascend the Butter Tubs Pass. After the summit at 1726 ft the drive descends into Wensleydale again. Proceed through the hamlet of Simonstone and in 1/2 mile reach a T-junction. From here a short detour to the right may be made to visit the 100 ft high waterfall of Hardraw Force. Access is via the Green Dragon Inn at Hardraw. *The main drive turns left, then takes the next turning right for the return to Hawes.*

Kisdon Force is a mass of tumbling falls and trees

Hardraw Force is a spectacular one hundred feet high

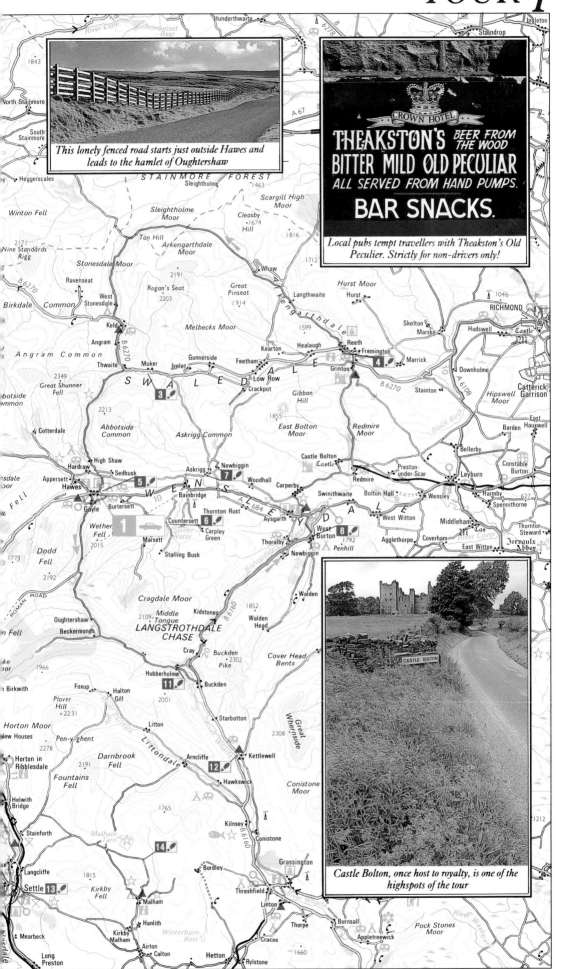

This lonely fenced road starts just outside Hawes and leads to the hamlet of Oughtershaw

Castle Bolton, once host to royalty, is one of the highspots of the tour

TOUR 2
67 MILES
Cove, Crag and Caverns

The serene priory ruins of Bolton Abbey in its romantic riverside setting and harsh lines on the horizon left by the lead mining industry are contrasting features that set the scene for this spectacular drive. Calling at Conistone, Arncliffe and other Dales villages the tour reaches beautiful Malham Tarn before returning to Skipton.

The drive starts from Skipton, a busy market town seated beside the River Aire and the Leeds-Liverpool canal. The most notable feature of the town is the castle dating in part from the 12th century. A Norman arch leads into the delightful sequestered Conduit Court with its feeling of timelessness. Other places of interest include the Craven Museum in the Town Hall, and the George Leatt Industrial and Folk Museum.

From the roundabout near the castle follow signs Harrogate (A59). In ½ mile turn left with the unclassified Embsay road. The former British Rail Station at Embsay is now the headquarters of the Yorkshire Dales Railway. *Near the end of the village turn left, signed Eastby and Barden. Pass through Eastby and ascend on to high ground from where there are good views. The drive then gradually descends into Wharfedale to reach the junction with the B6160. Here turn right, signed Bolton Abbey.* The Strid Wood Country Park lies to the left of the road before reaching Bolton Abbey (see page 36). Here the attractive 12th-century priory ruins stand beside the River Wharfe.

Continue to the Devonshire Arms at Bolton Bridge and turn left on to the A59, signed Harrogate. A climb is then made on to Blubberhouses Moor. *The drive enters a rocky valley before the descent into the Washburn Valley to Blubberhouses Church – at the head of the Fewston Reservoir. Here cross the river bridge and turn left on to an unclassified road, signed Pateley Bridge. This road crosses more high ground for some 7 miles before reaching the junction with the B6265 where the tour turns left, signed Grassington.* Disused lead workings can be seen on the left before passing the entrance to Stump Cross Caverns, once populated by wolverine, bison, fox and reindeer.

Remain on the B6265 and later pass through Hebden before entering Grassington (see page 42). This upper Wharfedale village contains a Yorkshire Dales National Park Centre. It is the main tourist spot in the area, with good shops and amenities. Exhibitions and festivals take place here in the summer months.

At Grassington go over the crossroads on to an unclassified road, signed Conistone. This pleasant by-road passes through attractive woodland and runs alongside the River Wharfe to the hamlet of Conistone (see page 39).

Here keep left, signed Kilnsey and Kettlewell, and cross the river bridge. On reaching the T-junction turn right on to the B6160 and shortly pass beneath the impressive Kilnsey Crag. After another ¾ mile turn left on to an unclassified road, signed Arncliffe. The drive now follows the valley of the River Skirfare to reach the grey stone village of Arncliffe (see page 32). Turn right, signed Litton and Halton Gill, and continue up the valley into Littondale. Pass through the hamlet of Litton and on to Halton Gill – an isolated farming settlement near the head of Littondale. Here turn left, signed Stainforth and Settle, and climb on to open moorland. This narrow, and occasionally gated, by-road reaches a height of over 1400 ft.

After 6 miles turn left, signed Malham. Cross more high ground and in 2¾ miles bear right. Half a mile farther go over the crossroads with the Grassington road and later pass the car parking area for Malham Tarn (NT). The actual tarn – or lake – lies to the left of the road and is a lonely sheet of water set within the moors at an altitude of 1229 ft. It can only be approached on foot. *Bear right, signed Malham, then descend and at the foot of the hill turn right for Malham (see page 52).* This pleasant village, on the Pennine Way footpath offers fine walks to two spectacular beauty spots – Malham Cove and Gordale Scar. The Cove (to the north of the village) is a limestone amphitheatre with cliffs nearly 300 ft high. Gordale Scar (to the north-east) is a wild defile containing waterfalls. In the village there is a Yorkshire Dales National Park Centre, where there is a good car park.

At the Buck Inn turn left and continue to Kirkby Malham. Here turn left with the Gargrave/Skipton road and follow the valley of the River Aire to Airton. In ¾ mile bear left and cross the river bridge, then pass through attractive countryside to reach Gargrave. Turn left on to the A65, still signed Skipton. In 2¾ miles, at the roundabout, take the second exit for the return to Skipton.

Kilnsey Crag dominates this part of Wharfedale

The towering cliffs and fallen boulders of Malham Cove

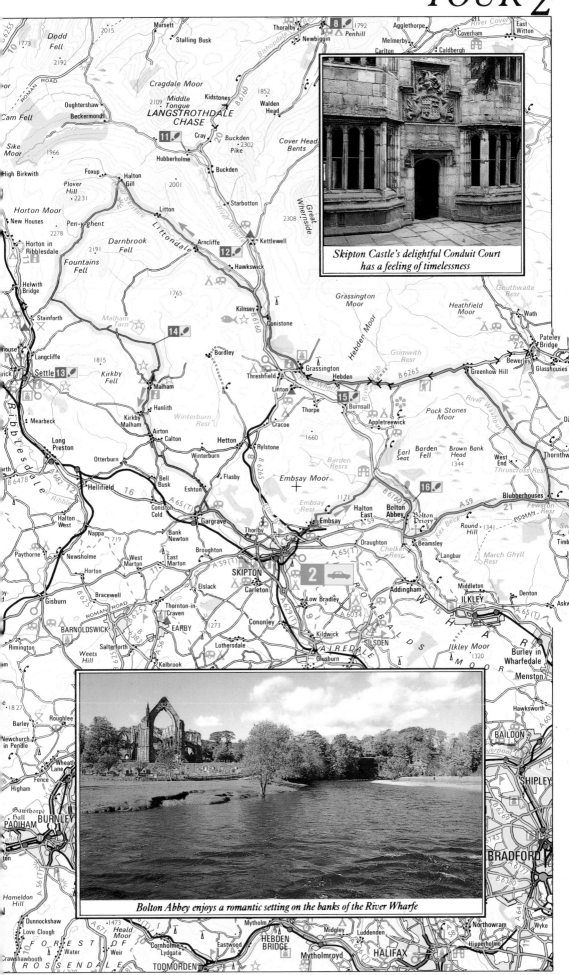

Skipton Castle's delightful Conduit Court has a feeling of timelessness

Bolton Abbey enjoys a romantic setting on the banks of the River Wharfe

WALK *1* Quaker Quest

Allow 3–3½ hours

This delightful but strenuous walk along the shins of the rolling Howgill Fells and the banks of the Lune, renowned for its salmon fishing, visits places of significance in the founding of the Religious Society of Friends.

Park at Sedbergh's Loftus Hill car park (SD658920). Diagonally opposite its entrance take the path along the churchyard. After the Civil War, a Leicestershire weaver's son, George Fox, dissatisfied with the established church travelled the land to seek a true church. In 1652 on Pendle Hill in Ribblesdale he had a vision of: 'a great people in white raiment by a river side, coming to the Lord; and the place that I saw them in was about Wensleydale and Sedbergh'. Soon after, on the day of Sedbergh Hiring Fair, he preached in this churchyard. A local sect called the Seekers shared his beliefs.

Continue along this path past Sedbergh School to its main gates. Across the road continue up between the houses and the cattle market, over another road, then up through Lockbank Farmyard to the fell gate. *Turn left and follow the steep wallside path, with splendid views, to a sunken walled lane on the left beyond the wood. Before going down this lane, 50m further on, notice the view of the Howgill Fells.*

Down the lane turn right along the road to Height of Winder Farm on the left. Take the footpath in front and round the outside of the house garden, through two field gates, then across the field as indicated by a fingerpost to a roadside stile. Cross the road, and keeping the same direction, cross a broken wall, then bear slightly right for a stile beside the electricity pole. The wallside path from here leads to High Branthwaite Farm. At the house fork left, go over a footbridge and up to the lane on the left to Draw Well Farm. This private residence, where George Fox stayed after his Sedbergh preaching, was an important early meeting place for the Quaker movement. Just above Draw Well Farm the path meets the Dales Way. **Turn left along the well-defined track past Low Branthwaite to join the River Lune at the disused railway viaduct, then follow riverside field paths to Lincoln's Inn Bridge. Walk with caution along the busy A684 to Ingmire Lodge, then by bridleway to the A683. Turn left, to Brigflatts down a lane to the right.* The story of Brigflatts is detailed in the Meeting House. One of the first, it was built in 1675.

From just above the hamlet an easy footpath across the meadows leads to Birks. Through this settlement a kissing gate on the right indicates the path back across the school playing fields to the church and the car park.

*A worthwhile extension is to follow the Dales Way right from Draw Well Farm to cross the River Lune below Hole House and ascend directly up Firbank Fell to Fox's Pulpit, the site of the vision's manifestation. Descend to New Field and take field paths to Lincoln's Inn Bridge. Allow an extra hour.

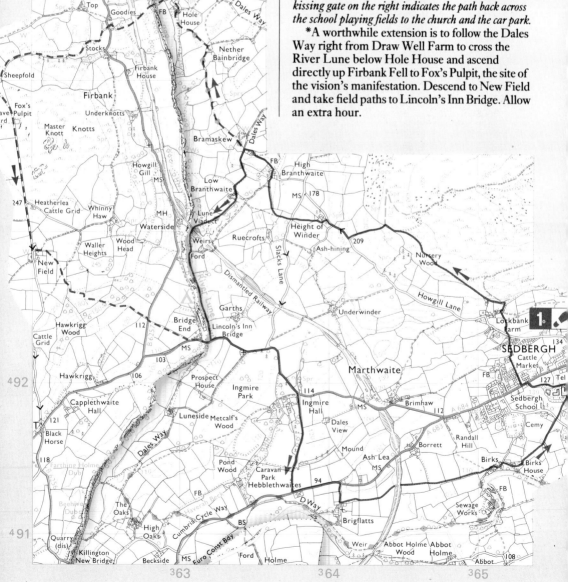

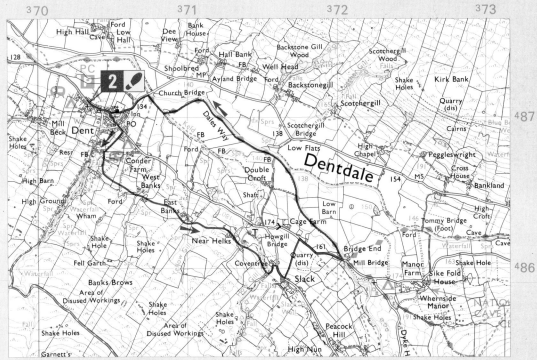

Delightful Dentdale

Allow 2–2½ hours

An easy walk from the picturesque village of Dent through lands settled by Norse farmers over 1000 years ago. A short sharp climb up a metalled road leads to easy field paths joining old farmsteads strung along the fellside commanding impressive views. The return route follows the attractive banks of Deepdale Beck and the River Dee.

Park at Dent car park (SD704871). Follow the cobbled street to the Adam Sedgwick memorial stone. Adam Sedgwick was born at Dent Parsonage in 1785. During 55 years as Professor of Geology at Trinity College, Cambridge, he had a profound influence on his specialised science. His pupils included Charles Darwin whose subsequent writings he violently opposed. He was a friend of Queen Victoria and Prince Albert, and a committed Dalesman, leaving for posterity a pamphlet that vividly illustrates life in Dentdale in the second half of the 19th century.

Turn right into another cobbled lane past the Post Office and Village Reading Room, then take the farm track over the cattle grid on the right. The metalled track goes past a modern bungalow and a second cattle grid to Throstle Hall. Behind, there are bird's eye views of the village and beyond the rolling Howgill Fells unfold.

An A-stile across the field to the left (south east) indicates the initial direction to be taken. Thereafter yellow disc markings on stiles, walls and barns draw the walker on in the same direction. The path leads in front of derelict West Banks, a splendid example of traditional Dales architecture, using local stone and timber, and adapting contemporary national designs to regional climatic considerations. From

A double porched dwelling in Dentdale

here upwards the valley follows the Norse settlement pattern of isolated farmsteads.

From West Banks the path passes above East Banks, then approaching East Helks descends to a concrete road through the farmyard in front of the house. The track then goes slightly right up to a stile on the left just before a barn, and diagonally across the pasture to the edge of the gill wood below. Along the wood, it descends to a footbridge, then in the guise of a narrow lane proceeds to meet the road at Coventree.

Follow the road up to a stile on the left opposite the cottage entrance, then the wall-side footpath to a second road below. Go along this road to the right for 300m, then take the riverside footpath on the left, signed Church Bridge, alongside Deepdale Beck and the River Dee back through Dent churchyard to the church and car park. The parish church, dedicated to St Andrew, founded in Norman times and probably maintained by the monks of Coverham Abbey, has seen many structural restorations. Worthy of note is the chancel floor of 'Dent Marble' – a hard limestone capable of being worked to a fine polish that reveals the intricate secret of worm-like fossil crinoids (sea-lilies) of its Carboniferous origins.

In the churchyard is the old grammar school where Adam Sedgwick's father, Richard, was schoolmaster as well as parish priest.

WALK 3
Superlative Swaledale

Allow 2¼ – 2¾ hours, or 1¾ – 2¼ hours

An easy two-part walk along the elevated flank of Ivelet Moor commanding exquisite aerial views of upper Swaledale, and back by tranquil riverside meadows.

Park carefully in Muker village, possibly near the old school (SD910978). A plaque on the school records as former pupils Richard and Cherry Kearton, the pioneer wildlife photographers.

Take the road up past the incongruous Literary Institute and the more traditional Public Hall, keeping the latter to your right and the post office to your left, to the start of the field path signed Gunnerside and Keld. The stiled path is unmistakable. At the apparent head of the valley and surrounded by lead mining disturbance, the derelict Crackpot Hall Farm stares blindly down.

A footbridge takes the path across the juvenile Swale to Ramps Holme. Turning to the right, the path forks after 200m. Follow the left hand track, signed Gunnerside via Road, to attain the tractor track from Ivelet Wood. A field gate immediately below leads Muker's Annual Fell Race competitors on to the fell side, whence they go directly up to Ivelet Boards over the skyline before a heady downhill fling back to the village showfield. The unfenced metalled road hereon affords spectacular views of Satron, Oxnop and Muker Sides across the dale, and behind, beyond Muker, the dark mass of Great Shunner Fell.

Above Calvert Houses an escape route runs steeply down to the riverside, but the extra kilometre to Gunnerside Lodge pays rich dividends at little additional effort. The valley is seen to widen into rich alluvial meadows enhanced by their filigree of white stone walls and embossed with numerous field barns. Gunnerside village tucked to one side sits comfortably in its natural setting with Brownsey Moor rising protectively behind. The bulk of Satron Side is broken by long white outcrops, the finest receding high up the wooded Oxnop Gill.

The road falls sharply to Gunnerside Lodge, perched like a majestic eagle enjoying a commanding prospect of the dale. Take the right fork steeply down past Ivelet, then along the riverside to Ivelet Bridge. This exquisite limestone bridge with its graceful arch is perhaps the most attractive in the area, despite the headless dog reputed to haunt it. The flat stone at its north eastern corner was where mourners once used to rest the coffins on the long 'Corpse Way' from the upper dale to burial in the only church, at Grinton.

From here a distinct and delightful path on the north bank of the river leads gently back to Ramps Holme Bridge, then by the outward route back to Muker.

Gunnerside Lodge enjoys breathtaking views of the dale

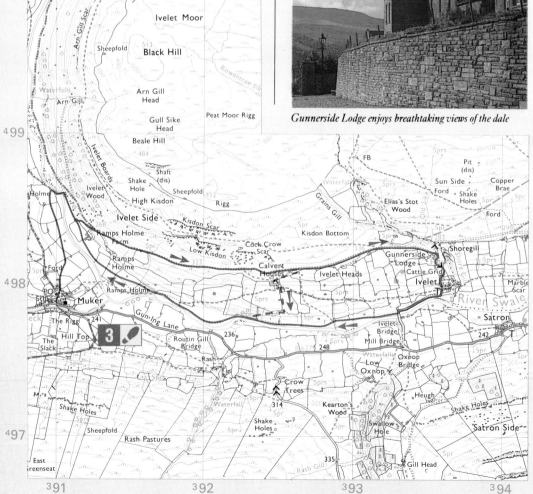

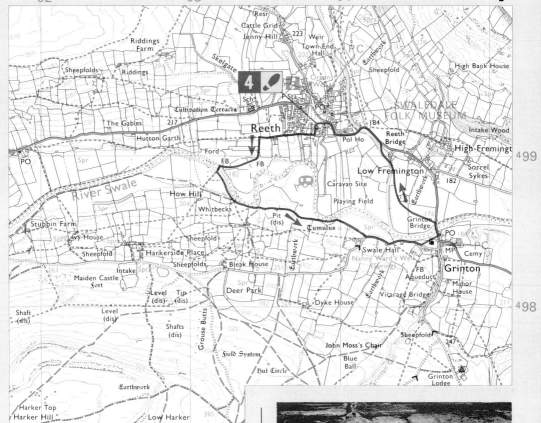

Riverside Ramble

Allow 1¾ hours

From the former lead mining capital of Swaledale, a leisurely riverside stroll along easy paths between Celtic earthworks to the 'Cathedral of the Dales', not many miles from where, in 627 AD, Paulinus converted the Angles and baptised them in the River Swale.

Park on the cobblestones at Reeth Green (SE038993). At the south side of the green take the narrow road between the Congregational Church and the Literary Institute to Back Lane. Turn right along this lane, bearing left at the fork. Across the river an ancient earthwork shows as a raised rampart stretching up the hillside. You will pass beside its foot. The map shows this, and other earthworks, including Maiden Castle (SE 022981), all believed to have been constructed by the Celtic Brigantes around 70 AD as defences against the Roman invaders.

At a fingerpost signed Harkerside and Grinton follow the lane downhill to the left, then the well-trodden path directly to the Reeth Suspension Bridge. (Sheet SE 09 indicates stepping stones). Cross the bridge, and follow the river's edge to the left. The view back across the river reveals Reeth Friends' School, now a primary school, founded by the Quaker Raw family in 1785. Around it, medieval cultivation terraces (lynchets) proclaim the town's Anglian antecedents in support of its Old English

Swaledale is scarred with the remains of lead mining

name which literally means 'stream' (Arkle Beck). The old tailings (spoil heaps) from lead mining exploitation on Fremington Edge, on the right of Arkengarthdale, are only just distinguishable from its limestone scars.

After the second stile, the track goes straight ahead while the river executes an extravagant bow to the left, to be rejoined a little further on before meeting the minor road and turning left to Swale Hall. 400m along the road enter the churchyard by the gate on the left. The Parish Church of St Andrew at Grinton was founded in the early 12th century. For 120 years it acted as an outlying mission of the Augustinian Priory at Bridlington. Scratches on the stonework around the porch show how retainers sharpened their arrows while their lords were at service.

Leave the churchyard by the path at its east end and turn left, noting the 17th-century Blackburn Hall opposite the Bridge Hotel. Over Grinton Bridge, a footpath on the left leads across the meadows. The Brigantian earthwork rises again from just north of here past the west side of the Georgian Draycott Hall.

The path continues past Fremington Mill, still retaining its mill race, a discarded mill stone, and out of sight the crumbling remains of its water wheel. Turn left at the road, and cross Reeth Bridge over Arkle Beck back to the green.

| 0 | 200 | 400 | 600 | 800 | 1 | | 2 | | 3 | Kilometres |
| 0 | 200 | 400 | 600 | 800 | 1000 | | | 1 | | 2 Miles |

SCALE 1:25 000

WALK 5
Along the Pennine Way

Allow 3–4 hours

A glimpse of picturesque Gayle, a long, steep ascent up the Old Cam Road between Hawes and Ribblehead to Dodd Fell's Ten End, and an exhilarating coast down the 20th-century's premier long distance footpath.

Start from Hawes National Park Centre car park (SD 876899). Walk up the village and take the steps and path up in front of Liverpool House between the church

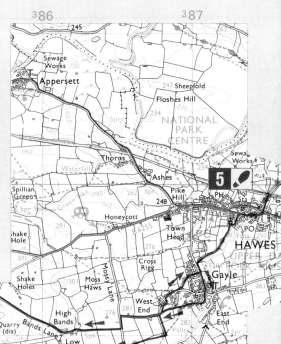

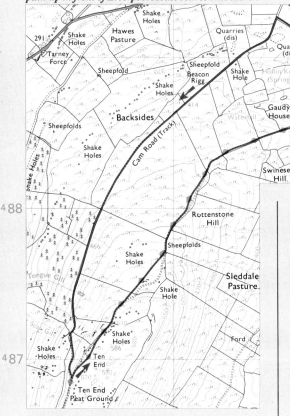

Hawes is a busy market town in Wensleydale

and the old schoolroom. Join the paved Pennine Way briefly to Gayle Lane, then follow the road left to Gayle Bridge. Towards Hawes, Gayle Beck flows over a fluted limestone bed past historic Gayle Mill and its mill race. In the opposite direction it descends its own broad staircase flanked by tall buildings to the left and attractive cottages to the right.

Go up Hargill, the cobbled lane in front of those cottages, along Gaits straight ahead through the village to the T junction. Turn left, then right along Bands Lane to the Old Cam Road. Go left up the track. The ascent up a stony tractor track affords splendid retrospective views of Hawes and Hardraw, with the Butter Tubs Pass bisecting Abbotside into Stags Fell to the east and Great Shunner Fell to the west. North west the long ridge of Cotter Fell recedes to the high 'Seats' of Mallerstang Edge, while due west Widdale Fell rises towards its summit at Great Knoutberry. On a clear day Whernside may be seen lurking beyond its southern flank. At the start of Snaizeholme Forest on the right, the outward and upward extent of the walk is heralded by the skyline ahead, soon to be graced by the sawn-off peak of Ingleborough.

A stone at the junction with a distinct path joined acutely declares the identity of the Pennine Way and points the return route to Hawes along a well defined track. The most striking feature of the descent, apart from the Pennine Way's extension beyond Hawes over Great Shunner Fell, is the view of the clear, stepped terraces of Wether Fell, their chequer of rectangular walled hay meadows looking for all the world like Asian paddy fields. It is interesting to reflect on some of the geographical names. Abbotside, like nearby Bishopdale, reminds us of the former influence of the monastic foundations. Wether Fell was where the monks fattened the wethers (castrated male lambs), Stags Fell where they grazed unbroken horses, not deer. Approaching Hawes two large industrial complexes compel the eye. The further one is Hawes Auction Mart where the locally bred livestock are traded. The nearer is the Wensleydale Creamery, home of the famous Wensleydale cheeses.

Superstition & Faith

Allow 2½ hours

Semerwater rise, Semerwater sink,
And swallow all save this li'le house
That gave me meat and drink. (Traditional)

A delightful easy walk, sometimes marshy in places, around an isolated upland lake steeped in legend and history, and incorporating visits to a Quaker Meeting House and a ruined church.

Park off the road at the foot of the lake (SD922876) near the large granite boulders known as the Carlow and Mermaid Stones. A giant once lived on Addlebrough, the flat-topped hill to the east. One day he had a fierce argument with the Devil, perched on top of Crag, the rough ridge to the west. The giant threw these stones, which fell short of their target to the lakeside. The Devil's response landed high on the flank of Addlebrough, where it can still be seen to the left of the wall.

Cross the bridge over the River Bain (England's shortest river) and climb up the steep hill, turning right at the top into Countersett. Past the former inn and Countersett Hall, take the path on the left to the Friends' Meeting House. Return to the crossroads and continue along the metalled Marsett Lane. The 'sett' ending of these two hamlets, and of Wensleydale's Appersett and Burtersett, is an old Norse word meaning hill pasture.

Across Marsett Bridge turn left along the track that follows the beck's natural fish nursery. Stalling Busk can be seen at the head of the lane. Stay on the lane over a footbridge then a ford to a stile by a barn on the left. (A footbridge slightly downstream offers a dry crossing and a sneaky little short cut!). The path follows a fairly level course through a chain of stiles to the ruined church. This building was erected in 1722 to replace an earlier erection of 1603. In its turn, it was replaced in 1909 by a modern church in Stalling Busk.

The path now nears the lake, and stirs thoughts of its legendary and historic past. Once, some two thousand years ago, an old man visiting the prosperous township that existed hereabouts, begged in vain for food and shelter from its proud inhabitants. Only in the last poor cottage, high up on a hillside, did an elderly couple take him in for the night. Next morning he uttered the curse that heads this piece. The earth opened, and a great flood came to wipe away the village, sparing only his elderly hosts. And now, on many a still dark night, can be heard the wails of the drowned and the muffled tolling of the old town's bells! Disbelief should be tempered by caution. A particularly dry summer exposed the bed of the lake to reveal the foundations of a late Bronze Age village raised on piles over the water as protection against wild animals. In addition, among other prehistoric finds was a beautiful bronze spear head, now displayed in the Upper Dales Folk Museum at Hawes.

The road beside High Blean marks the end of the path, from which an easy few minutes' walk will take you back to the car.

SCALE 1:25 000

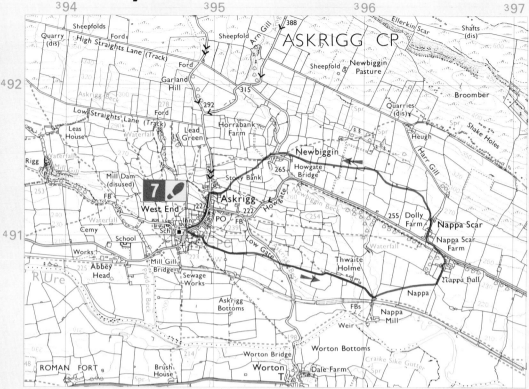

Fortified Farmhouse

Allow 1½ hours

An easy leisurely stroll past an imposing fortified farmhouse, through sleepy hamlets and peaceful meadows in historic Askrigg, intimately revealed in *Yorkshire Village* **by Marie Hartley and Joan Ingilby.**

Park in Askrigg market place near the church (SD948910). Note the market cross with its adjacent iron ring set into the cobbles to tether bulls for baiting by dogs, and the homogeneous mix of buildings of all sizes and ages.

Opposite the market cross, take the lane alongside the 3-storied watershot 'Cringley', a residential home sometimes masquerading under a more familiar title – *'Skeldale House'!* Where in *All Creatures Great and Small* have we heard that before?

This leads to a narrow walled lane with Penhill looming ahead like some bulky ziggurat and Addlebrough sitting squatly to the far right. *At the end of the lane, a stile on the right gives access to a field path* continuing on the same line to the Worton road. *Across this road, take the left fork to the bridge and ford at the entrance to Nappa House.* At this point the stile to the left of the barn leads the walker towards a gate diagonally across the field. By now it is possible to make out the glacial moraines and drumlins of the valley bottoms, as well as the limestone escarpments stepped along their sides.

At the next field gate, turn left up the track to Nappa Hall. It was his bravery at Agincourt in 1415 that earned James Metcalfe of Worton the gift of the Nappa estate. He completed alterations to the hall in 1459, and for 300 years thereafter it remained

the seat of the locally powerful Metcalfes. Its older, crenellated western tower with its kitchen and pantry on the ground floor follows the style of a typical Norman keep. The two-storied eastern tower and separating hall, completed in 1459, added comfort and style. Standing virtually unaltered from its original conception, Nappa Hall is a unique example of a 14th- and 15th-century defensive stone house. Remember that this is a private residence and a working farm, so please respect the occupant's privacy.

At the road above the hall go left for 120m, then turn up the metalled road on the right. Immediately beyond the last house and barn of the hamlet of Nappa Scar take the stile to the left. After an initial diagonal uphill slant, the path continues along the high sides of the fields past the front of two barns. On the opposite side of the valley the long shallow scar woods typify Wensleydale scenery, while beyond Bainbridge fort the Roman road strikes an unerring straight line over the southern shoulder of Wether Fell.

A succession of stiles gives way to field gates approaching the tiny village green of Newbiggin. Across the green and over the bridge into the lane, a stile on the left takes the path diagonally across the corner of the first field to be led by a number of stiles down Stony Bank into upper Askrigg. *The last house on the right before the fell road* is subject of *Yorkshire Cottage* by Ella Pontefract and Marie Hartley.

From here the road strays past interesting old buildings and intriguing alleys back to the starting point in the market place.

Harvesting peat in Wensleydale

Crusaders' Chapel

Allow 2½–3 hours

An airy upland walk with magnificent views of mid Wensleydale to the mysterious ruins of the Crusaders' Chapel, with its tiny stone coffins, on the flanks of historic Penhill.

Park carefully beside (not on) West Burton village green (SE017867). At the bottom of the green, take the track to the right past the old mill to a packhorse bridge and a spectacular waterfall. Cross the bridge and follow a well-trodden footpath up to a stile, marked with a yellow disc, at the corner of Barrack Wood. Turning right over the stile, the path heads straight up to the right of Knarlton Knot, then as it becomes less steep, south-eastwards towards a fingerpost in the wall at the entrance to the disused Hudson's Quarry. Follow the quarry road left to join Morpeth Gate above Morpeth Scar. *The gentle airy descent down the quarry road affords extensive views up Waldendale, Bishopdale and Wensleydale. The long riggs (ridges) sloping evenly down between the tributary valleys to the major dale below illustrate clearly the effects of glacial sculpturing.*

The lane, now known as High Lane, winds round the broad terrace below Dove Scar. A walled lane on the left leads down towards Swinithwaite below and 14th-century Bolton Castle across the valley. Bolton Castle's main claim on history relates to the six months in 1568–69 when it served as prison to Mary, Queen of Scots.

Where the track, now concreted, swings sharp right, go left across the field between two plantations. In the bottom right hand corner, a field gate gives access to, and sight of, the ruined Crusaders' Chapel across the next field. The Order of the Knights Templars or Poor Knights of Christ and the Temple of Solomon was established in the mid 12th century. A military order under strict religious rule, it existed to protect Christians on pilgrimage to the Holy Land. It was donated great wealth which it efficiently administered as international financier and banker. Its power and influence engendered much suspicion and resentment that culminated in its suppression in the early 14th century. This chapel, built around 1200 AD, was used by them for a little over a century until its transfer on dissolution to the Knights Hospitallers. In ruins for over 300 years, it was uncovered in 1840.

From the chapel cross the lane and follow a level grassy path above Spring Bank Wood. (Quiet parties may be rewarded with a glimpse of one of its resident roe deer). Beyond a gate in line with the path, it descends to a slightly lower level before emerging on to Morpeth Gate. Follow the lane down to the foot of Barrack Wood. Go through the wood over the stile on the left, then back by the outward route.

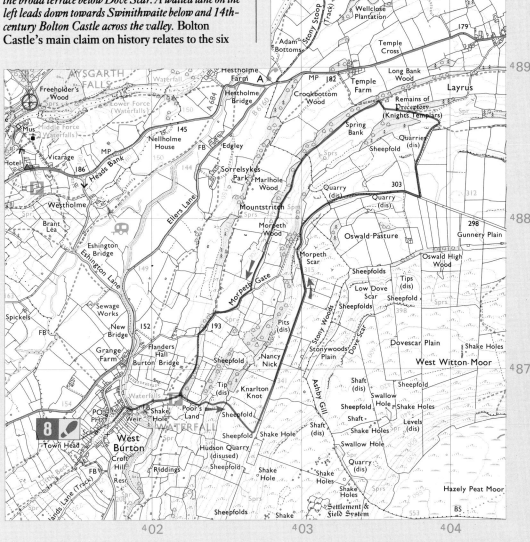

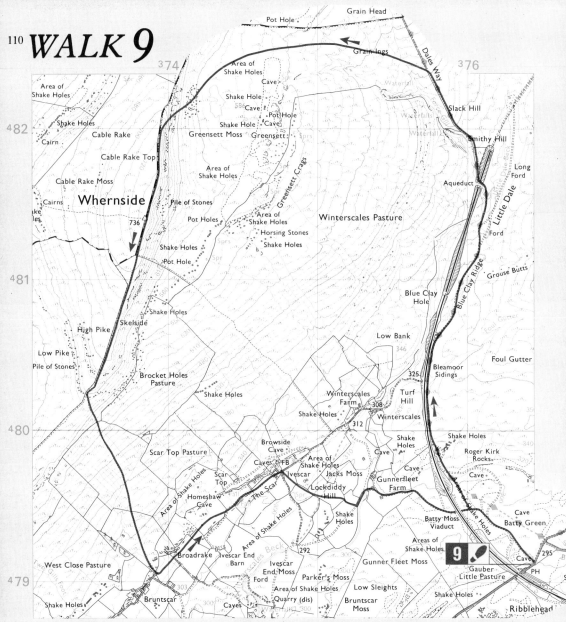

Tarns & Tops

Allow 4–5 hours

A demanding ascent, by the easiest route, to Yorkshire's highest peak (2415ft), with an intriguing introduction to some of the engineering miracles of the Settle-Carlisle railway. Boggy in places, stony and steep in others, this route should not be undertaken lightly, or without boots, windproof and waterproof clothing, and possibly spare rations. Map and compass should be carried. In mist, only experienced walkers and map readers should consider it.

Park near the Station Inn, Ribblehead (SD764791). Take the track towards the viaduct, breaking right just before the arches to follow the line side past Bleamoor signal box to the bridge and aqueduct just before Bleamoor tunnel. The 72 mile long Settle-Carlisle Railway was built by the Midland Railway Company between 1869 and 1875. During its construction a number of shanty towns with improbable names like Belgravia, Inkerman, Jericho, Jerusalem, Salt Lake City and Sebastopol housed the navvies and often their families in this extreme region. The design and construction of

the 24 span, 100ft high viaduct, the graceful aqueduct and the trim bridges are of the highest standard. The line disappearing into the 2629 yard long tunnel can be traced by the spoil heaps and air shafts strung over the moor top. Later it can be followed sweeping round Dent Fell to disappear again into long Rise Hill Tunnel.

Across the railway the track known as Craven's Old Way sweeps gently up the eastern flank of Whernside. The attractive waterfall of Force Gill below Slack Hill makes an excellent picnic place. 300m before the wall ahead, a stile to the left leads in a gentle arc from Grain Ings to the edge of Greensett Tarn. Some of the peat haggs reveal at their bases well-preserved twigs of birch trees from over 5000 years ago.

Just beyond the boulder-strewn shoulder of Whernside the path strikes diagonally upwards towards the nick in the skyline, then follows the wall along Cable Rake Top to the 2415ft summit's Ordnance Survey trig point.

Follow the summit wall past the unpleasant and dangerous direct descent to Ribblehead. After a gentle but invigorating 1500m ridge walk a cairn below the second steep stony section indicates the route down to the Bruntscar Lane. When reached, turn left and follow the bridleway in front of Broadrake Farm to Ivescar. A little way down the lane to its front, a stile on the left takes a footpath diagonally across the field then by wall sides to the farm road by Winterscales Beck. Go left, take the first track on the right over a bridge, then under Ribblehead viaduct back to the Station Inn.

Geological Gleanings

Allow 3–3½ hours

A bracing upland walk along old bridleways up carboniferous Clapdale, down Silurian and Ordovician Crummackdale, to the peculiar Norber erratics. An interesting walk for the amateur geologist.

Park at Clapham National Park Centre car park (SD745693). Turn right out of the car park, up the village. At the church, take the lane to the right signed Austwick. At the corner of Thwaite Plantation turn left into Long Lane, signed Selside. To the right (east) the North Craven Fault can be seen stretching away below Norber. Ahead and to the right the long cliffs and screes of Thwaite Scars exhibit the products of past glacial and present climatic erosion. The valley below reveals the entrances to subterranean drainage systems, particularly Ingleborough and Foxholes caves.

At the end of the walled lane a clear broad green track heads just below a large cairn on the skyline ahead. In Clapham Bottoms to the left, low rudimentary walls outline ancient field systems, while sink holes indicate the presence of eroded limestone below the overlying drift.

At a point where the lion couchant of Pen-y-ghent just appears ahead, another bridleway joins from the right. Turn along this springy turf track passing below a band of limestone pavement (not shown on map), then past Crummackdale Farm for the road to Austwick. Below, the squat wooded shape of Oxenber with its iron-age settlement on top and its Anglian lynchets frilling its skirt beckons the walker on.

As the road sweeps sharply right beyond Sowerthwaite Farm entrance, a stile on the right, signed Norber, leads to Nappa Scars. Notice the breccias between the base of the Great Scar limestone and the much older Ordovician rocks.

Continue westwards through a stile on to the open fell. The Norber erratics are dispersed just a little higher up. The Norber erratics are large boulders of Silurian rocks uplifted by glaciers from Crummackdale and deposited on the limestone shelves of Norber Brow. Erosion of the limestone by wind and weather is believed to explain the slender blocks that serve as pedestals to these massive boulders.

From the wall below Norber Brow follow the footpath past the foot of Robin Proctor's Scar, then diagonally across the field, skirting an old mere to the right, to Thwaite Lane, thence back to Clapham.

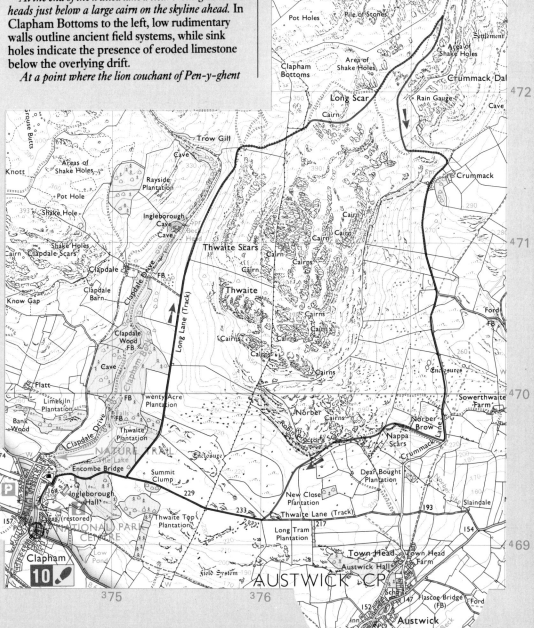

WALK 11
Pastoral Paradise

Allow 2 hours

A little gem of a walk in idyllic surroundings. Its easily gained altitude affords panoramic views of Langstrothdale Chase, a former hunting forest, and of upper Wharfedale's stepped hillsides and small lush meadows. The gentle descent is by the banks of Cray Gill to the fascinating church.

Park along the quiet road over the bridge beside Hubberholme Church (SD926783). From the field gate next to the church, walk up the drive to Scar House. The view up Langstrothdale gradually unfolds to reveal bright pastures studded with limestone boulders and rugged outcrops, with hanging woods clinging to the hillsides along the rich limey escarpments. Hubberholme, once Hubergheham, is an Anglian name meaning the homestead of Hunburg, a women's name. Its holme ending suggests a Viking adaptation. Scar House with its two datestones, 1698 and 1876, has seen many alterations, but its sturdy construction from local stone, its mullioned windows and its stone slab

A traditional Dales barn at Starbotton in Wharfedale

roof with kneelers above the strengthening quoins, set it clearly in the Dales tradition.

The path weaves between the house and barn, then turns sharply right up a few limestone rocks on to the soft, springy turf. It stays at this level right along the top of Hubberholme Wood. The wood consists primarily of indigenous trees – ash and wych elm interspersed with hazel, holly and blackthorn, with a sprinkling of oaks and sycamores. Gradually Buckden Pike appears ahead, and the long glacially-widened valley of the Wharfe emerges from the screen of trees, revealing the villages of Buckden and Starbotton melting modestly into their surroundings. After a while a limestone pavement is passed. Its grikes, havens for a variety of flowers from the ever-nibbling sheep, all follow similar geometric directions. Its clints, the intermediary blocks, stand barrenly in sculptured brilliance.

Crook Gill is crossed by a footbridge, after which the path rises slightly, past the front of a barn, to culminate beyond a farmyard in the hamlet of Cray. Cray is an old British river name aptly meaning 'clean and fresh'. Its village inn, in accordance with regional practice, offers morning coffee, lunchtime snacks and evening meals, but not afternoon tea.

The return journey retraces the outward through the farmyard, bearing left in front of the last cottage to descend to Cray Gill. Following the gill with its numerous cataracts, the path crosses tributary Crook Gill by an old packhorse bridge. The word gill, like beck, is Norse in origin, and refers to a ravine or narrow valley. The gill bed, often cut deep into the limestone rock, is seen studded with potholes and displaying many fossils.

The gillside path joins the quiet road at How Ings. It is only a short distance along to the right to Hubberholme Church. The church will unfold its own wonders to the curious visitor, but features to look out for include its rare musicians' rood loft dated 1558, its unusual font, and the mice running up and down the ends of the pews!

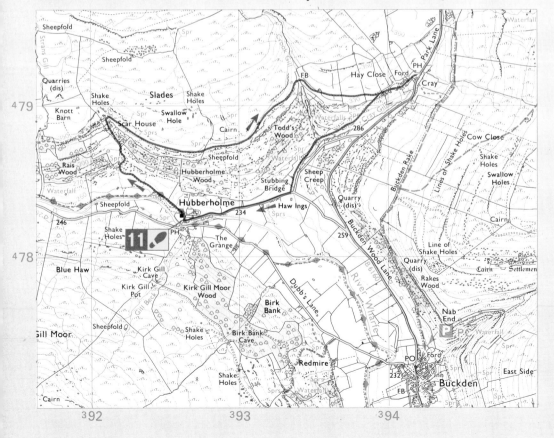

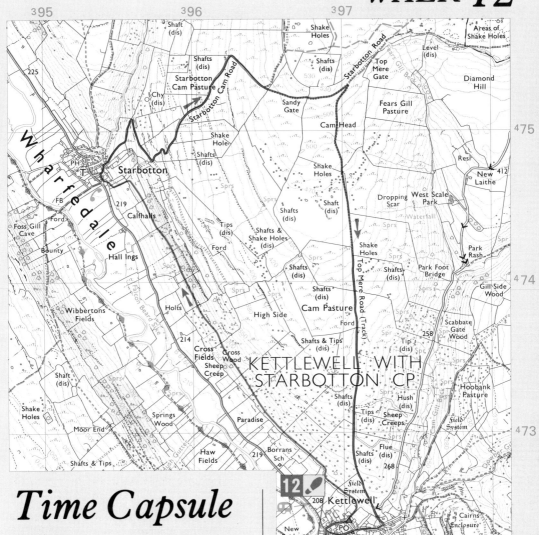

Time Capsule

Allow 3–4 hours, 1½–2 for soft option!

Celtic fortifications fifty years older than Hadrian's Wall, Roman highways, Anglian and Viking settlements, monastic drove roads, Elizabethan pack routes, three centuries of lead mining depredation and 25 centuries of agricultural landscaping – these are some of the features of this intriguing and inspiring journey into history. Walking boots or stout shoes, and windproof clothing are recommended at all seasons.

Park at Townfoot Bridge car park, Kettlewell (SD967723). Cross the small bridge into the village, and follow the road up the left side of the Bluebell Hotel. Where the road turns right, go straight ahead, over a stile, then turn left along the wall-side. The path continues roughly at this level all the way to Starbotton. Kettlewell is an Anglian name meaning a bubbling spring. The route you are travelling follows the line of a Roman road from Ilkley, up Wharfedale over Stake Pass to Bainbridge in Wensleydale, and on to Catterick. The track sloping diagonally up the opposite side of the dale led to the Moor End lead mines.

At the third barn (Calfhalls) after the wood, angle left down to Starbotton village. Here, Grandma and the toddlers might justifiably cross the road (B6160) and follow the very attractive and well signposted Dales Way back to Kettlewell. Sturdier souls will bear right through the village past the mullioned cottage dated

1656 to a walled track on the right winding steeply up the hillside – Starbotton Road. At an airy 1600 feet where the walled lane (and the climb) ends, a stile admits to a springy turf path with Great Whernside looming ahead and mid Wharfedale exposing itself like some gigantic three-dimensional map. Almost unexpectedly, as a track goes off to the right, the peak of Little Whernside reveals itself left ahead, and much nearer, the semi-amphitheatre of Ta Dyke, commanding the head of the tributary valley to the north east of Kettlewell. Ta Dyke, constructed by the native Brigantes around 70 AD to prevent Roman penetration via Coverdale into Wensleydale, consists of a ditch and earth bank strategically constructed over a mile of natural limestone escarpment.

Extra time should be allowed for a diversionary close examination, but the descent to Kettlewell should be taken from this point, where a green track courses straight down the ridge to the right. The incredible views down Wharfedale including the gleaming limestone terraces of Langcliffe more than repay the sweat of the ascent. At the gate to the walled lane, note the lead mining bell pits to the left, and just before the second gate, on the same side, the top of the old flue from the lead smelting mill in the valley below. The track, Top Mere Road, joins the metalled Park Rash Road just above Kettlewell, and a choice of downhill lanes lead back to the car park.

0	200	400	600	800	1		2		3	Kilometres

0	200	400	600	800	1000		1		2 Miles

SCALE 1:25 000

WALK 13
Rambling
Ribble

Allow 2 – 2½ hours

A gentle, easy walk along sheltered old lanes, through flowery pastures and varied woodland, commanding extensive views of mid Ribblesdale and adjacent Lancashire.

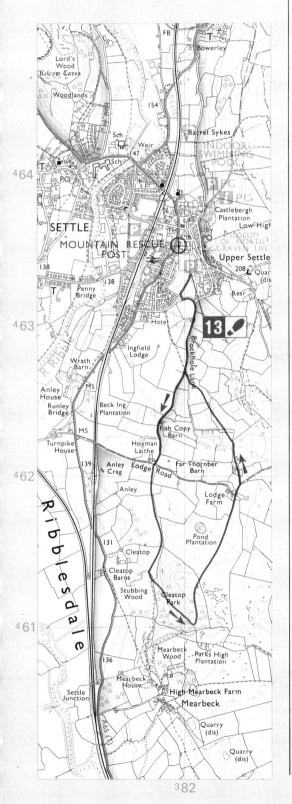

Butter-making at Lodge Hall in Ribblesdale. The art is still practised in a number of Dales kitchens

Park in Settle's Greenfoot car park (SD821632), best approached from the A65 at the southern end of Settle, turning into Butch Lane immediately north of the prominent Falcon Hotel. It is 400m along this lane on the left hand side. From the car park entrance walk 100m left along Butch Lane, then take the walled path on the right signed Mearbeck. Beyond the garden allotments to the left, the terracing of the fields is a relic of medieval strip farming. Each strip, called a lynchet, was of a size able to be tilled by a man and his ox-drawn wooden plough in one day. It was believed to be sufficient to sustain a good husbandman, his wife and two children, with grains and pulses throughout the year. They were often one furrow long – the derivation of 'furlong'.

At the end of the walled lane, beside Hayman Laithe (laithe = barn), cross Lodge Lane and follow field paths (in single file) indicated by stiles, to the corner of Cleatop Park. As Cleatop Park is approached, the retrospective view is impressive. Below it is not difficult to envisage the vast lake that existed after the Ice Ages. At its nearest edge, the valley is flanked by the railway, its man-made straight lines contrasting with the natural meaningless meanderings of the River Ribble. Here the railway can be seen diverging to Lancaster and the west, and by the famous Settle-Carlisle line to the north. The south western horizon is dominated by the dark, heathery Bowland Hills of Lancashire, while to the north the white limestone of Giggleswick Scar and Settle's Castleberg cliff frame the rugged splendour of Pen-y-ghent.

Continue below this mixed wood to enter by the gate half way along. Follow the diagonal path up through the wood to meet another path joining from a small footbridge on the right. Cleatop Park is an old wood now owned by the Yorkshire Dales National Park. It has a wide range of species of different ages, and is host to an extensive variety of woodland plants and birds. In places, clusters of upright, pole-like growth from gnarled stumps reveal the ancient woodland craft of coppicing. This system of woodland management, based on a 7–10 year cutting cycle, provided the ideal material for making sheep hurdles. It also ensured a steady firewood supply without killing off the trees.

Our path takes a dog leg to the left, up through the pine trees to leave the north eastern side of the wood by a small gate. Head across the rough pasture to the field gate just to the right of Lodge Farmhouse. Turn right along the lane for 100m, then take the walled lane on the left. A clearly defined path now angles down across fields to Mearbeck Lane where the walk started. Turn right and retrace the outward track back to the Greenfoot car park.

Mire, Moor & Tarn

Allow 2–3 hours

An airy upland stroll in historic limestone country to Great Close Mire, Malham Moor and Tarn, sanctuaries for a wide range of waders and moorland birds, and to the Malham Tarn Nature Trail. Easy walking. A leaflet describing the nature trail is available at Ha Mire and Water Houses.

Park at Street Gate (SD903656). Lock up securely. Like you, car thieves are often attracted to quiet, lonely places! Walk up the metalled road beside the wall towards Great Close Scar (left) and Great Close Mire (right). Great Close Mire, a former glacial tarn whose shores were once frequented by hunters and fishermen of the Middle Stone Age, is believed to have been drained in historic time. It still retains a swampy character and is host to many rare and interesting plants and birds.

The road continues past Middle House Farm to Middle House, the site of an old building to house the Fountains Abbey shepherds. To the right, below Middle House, are its old crofts surrounded by a maze of very ancient walls – possibly the oldest stone walls in the area.

Just before Middle House Farm and a little short of the ancient walls, a stile on the left leads across West Great Close to the edge of Malham Tarn. Malham Tarn, a natural lake, sits on a bed of Silurian slate on the edge of the North Craven Fault, its waters held back by a moraine of glacial debris. At one time it belonged to Fountains Abbey, whose monks valued its stocks of succulent trout. It is nowhere more than 4¼m deep.

The nature trail follows the track on the north shore

of the tarn past Tarn House. Toilets are provided for walkers at the side of the track behind the House. Now owned by the National Trust, Malham Tarn House is an important Field Study Centre of the Field Studies Council, and offers residential courses of both scientific and general nature throughout the year. It was built in 1852 on the site of a former building as a shooting lodge for the estate owners, the Listers of Gisburn.

The nature trail continues past Tarn Moss, an acid peat bog once part of the tarn, to the Victorian estate cottages and the imposing 17th-century farmhouse of Water Houses. This old building, datestone 1635, no longer a farmhouse, is in excellent preservation and a good example of vernacular architecture.

The trail ends here. It is possible to continue the walk by metalled roads past Higher Tren House and Water Sinks Gate back to Street Gate. But a more congenial route, strongly to be recommended, is to retrace one's steps through the nature trail to its official start at the corner of Ha Mire Plantation, then by the Tarn House road back to Street Gate.

WALK 15 Winding Wharfedale

Allow 2 hours, 2½ with church visit.

A pleasant country ramble involving an easy ascent rewarded by splendid views, a chance to visit a beautiful historic church with Anglian and Viking features, and a riverside perspective of two contrasting faces of the River Wharfe.

The walk starts at Hebden village (SE027629). Park in the broad street near the old school, and take the descending footpath just beyond it. After the footbridge follow the finger-post signed Hartlington Raikes across a rough track to a stile to the left of the field gate. Cross the next field diagonally to the right hand corner of Ranelands Farm. Through the farmyard's three gates the path continues in roughly the same direction. On this short sharp ascent you may be glad of the excuse to stop and admire the view behind. Hebden village nestles comfortably above its beck with Grassington Hospital beyond. The River Wharfe trickles gently down from Linton, and on its opposite banks the limestone reef knolls of Elbolton and Kail Hill jauntily assert themselves at the foot of the more substantial Thorpe Fell.

A field gate in the top right hand corner of the field extends the path, rising gently, towards a fingerpost at the wallside above the field gate. Follow this wall to the

left to the A-style at its top right hand corner. This is the highest point of the walk, and Burnsall village begins to emerge to the right below.

Follow the path, crossing two more A stiles, to the A stile opposite South View Farm on Hartlington Raikes (road). Do not cross the stile, but follow the path at right-angles indicated by the fingerpost signed Burnsall. It descends through hay meadows, the route indicated by stiles marked with yellow discs to Skuff Road. The stile immediately opposite leads down to the riverside and Burnsall Bridge. Some may wish to follow the riverside path northwards from immediately across the bridge. The more curious will meander up the village past the chapel and old grammar school to visit the church. Burnsall Parish Church is dedicated to St Wilfrid who visited the settlement around 700 AD. Of particular interest are its pre-Norman sculptures, especially the fragments of Anglo-Danish grave covers; some still bearing traces of their original paint, its Anglo-Danish font, and its rare Viking hogback tombstones.

A path just above the church leads down to the riverside, and continues past Wilfrid Scar to Loup Scar. Here the river has cut a deep channel through the limestone rock to leave contorted cliffs to the sides and a narrow course of turbulent water swirling erratically over deeply-rounded potholes in its bed. A very little distance beyond, it resumes its more customary local demeanour of calm, unhurried flow.

The path continues to the Hebden Suspension Bridge. After negotiating its tremulous crossing the path goes straight ahead to Mill Lane. Across Mill Bridge to the right, the footpath on the left leads back between two modern bungalows and ultimately over Hebden Beck, back to the old school and village.

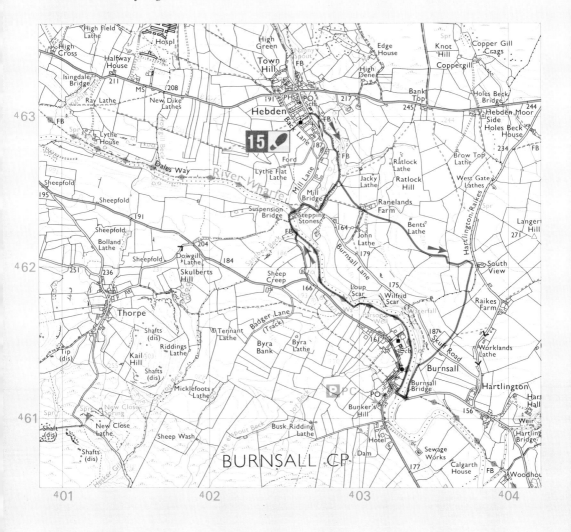

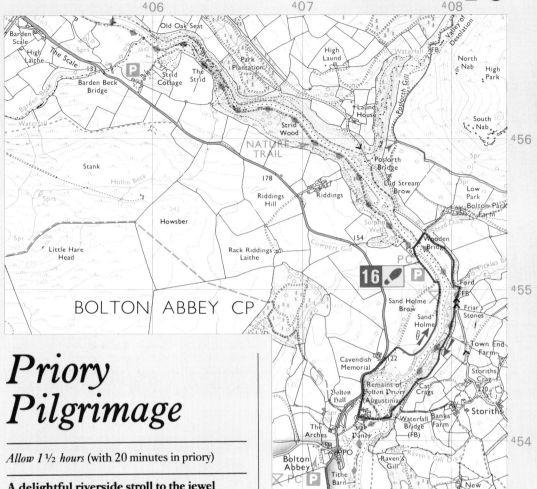

Priory Pilgrimage

Allow 1½ hours (with 20 minutes in priory)

A delightful riverside stroll to the jewel in the crown of the Yorkshire Dales – the ancient priory of Bolton in Wharfedale. There is a detective puzzle for children, and the optional adventure of a wide river crossing by stepping stones.

Park at the riverside carpark (Cavendish Pavilion) just north of Bolton Abbey (SE078552). The station around which the village grew was wrongly named by an official of the railway company. Here is a priory, not an abbey, but the name sticks!

Cross the narrow bridge opposite the café. Take the path on your right to the ford. 50m up the road beyond the ford, take the clear footpath to your right. There are other paths, but this one offers the best views of the river and priory. A spectacular aspect of Bolton Priory soon reveals itself in dignified dilapidation. Beyond it Bolton Hall, shooting lodge of the Dukes of Devonshire, is built round the 14th-century priory gatehouse, and to its left can be seen the high wall that surrounded the priory. The outlines of the former fishponds can just be made out astride the path leading to Bolton Abbey village beyond.

The path descends to a sturdy footbridge across the River Wharfe. Adventurous spirits will take up the challenge of the alternative stepping stones. Bolton Priory was built from 1155 onwards by the religious order of Augustinian Canons. Despite their black monastic dress, the canons were not monks. They were ordained priests whose mission was to go out daily into the surrounding area preaching the gospel and ministering to the needs of the people. The dissolution by Henry VIII of all religious foundations between 1536 and 1539 was not allowed to interrupt this function, since the priory nave has continued to this day as the parish church. Its last leader, Prior Moone, started building a tower at its west entrance in 1520. The dissolution interrupted its completion. After 463 years as a ruin the tower was eventually roofed over. High inside are the sculptured busts of Prior Moone and his present-day successor as priest-in-charge, Canon Maurice Slaughter.

PUZZLE. Which famous nursery rhyme was made up here?
CLUES. 1. The name of the last prior.
        2. Mistress Hey, a neighbour in continuous dispute with him over land boundaries.
Voluntary guides may help you to solve it or confirm your answer.

From the west door, take the drive north, up to the road, then the footpath along the top of the river bank to the Cavendish Memorial at the top of the road to the car park – a drinking fountain in memory of Lord Frederick Cavendish, brutally murdered in 1882. The path slopes gently down to the picnic area and car park at the riverside.

If time allows, follow the nature trail to the famous Strid, a deep narrow gorge studded with potholes and a succession of menacing whirlpools. Although stony, this path is passable for wheelchairs and pushchairs.

Index

Other Ordnance Survey Maps of the Yorkshire Dales

How to get there with the Routemaster and Tourist Series
Reach the Yorkshire Dales from Manchester, Leeds or Carlisle and other parts of Northern England with Sheet 5
NORTHERN ENGLAND of the ROUTEMASTER SERIES.

Exploring with the Landranger and Outdoor Leisure Maps

Landranger Series
1¼ inches to one mile or 1:50 000 scale

These maps cover the whole of Britain and are good
for local motoring and walking. Each contains
tourist information such as parking, picnic places,
viewpoints and rights of way. Sheets covering the
Yorkshire Dales are:

91   Appleby-in-Westmorland and surrounding
      area
92   Barnard Castle and surrounding area
98   Wensleydale & Upper Wharfedale
99   Northallerton, Ripon and surrounding area
103   Blackburn, Burnley and surrounding area
104   Leeds, Bradford & Harrogate area

Outdoor Leisure Series
2½ inches to one mile or 1:25 000 scale

These maps for walkers show the countryside of
Britain in great detail, including field boundaries and
rights of way in England and Wales.
The maps with the walks in this book are extracted from
the Outdoor Leisure Maps of the Yorkshire Dales.
There are three sheets in the series:

Yorkshire Dales   (showing Malham, Central
Wharfedale, Ribblesdale and part of the National Park)
Yorkshire Dales   (showing Wensleydale, Swaledale
and part of the National Park)
Yorkshire Dales   (showing Whernside, Ingleborough
and Pen-y-ghent and part of the National Park)

Acknowledgements

The publishers would like to thank the many individuals and organisations who helped in the preparation of this book. Special thanks are due to Dr Christopher Wood and Tim Haley of the Yorkshire Dales National Park Centre at Grassington, and the National Park Area Wardens.

The publishers also gratefully acknowledge the following for the use of their photographs and illustrations:

P & G Bowater

EA Bowness

Mary Evans Picture Library

Laurie Fallows

John Fell

John Forder

The Green Howards Regimental Museum, Richmond

Marie Hartley & Joan Ingliby

EA Janes Nature Photographers

KAG Design

Matt Kirby

Colin Molyneux

National Railways Museum, York

Richmondshire Museum

D Ronsall Nature Photographers

Skipton Castle

Theakston's Brewery

David Thomas

Turner painting reproduced by courtesy of the British Museum

Wensleydale Creameries

Harry Williams

Geoffrey Wright

Malcolm Wright

AA Publications Division Photographic Library